# Introduction



When I started freesciencelessons in 2013, I had one simple g[...] their understanding of science. When I was at school (and we'r[...] now), science was always my favourite subject. It's not surprising that I w[...] become a science teacher. I know that many students find science challenging. But I really believe that this doesn't have to be the case. With patient teaching and a bit of hard work, any student can make amazing progress.

Back in 2013, I had no idea how big freesciencelessons would become. The channel now has nearly 70 million views from 192 countries with a total view time of over 300 years. I love to hear from the students who have patiently watched the videos and realised that they can do science after all, despite in many cases having little confidence in their ability. And just like in 2013, I still make all the videos myself (many students think that I have a staff of helpers, but no, it's just me).

This workbook is designed to complement the Biology 1 videos for the AQA specification. However, there is a huge amount of overlap with other exam boards and in the future I'll be making videos and workbooks for those as well. I've packed the workbook full of questions to help you with your science learning. You might decide to start at the beginning and answer every question in the book or you might prefer to dip in and out of chapters depending on what you want to learn. Either way is fine. I've also written very detailed answers for every question, again to help you really develop your understanding. You can find these by scanning the QR code on the front of the book or by visiting freesciencelessons.co.uk/b1cshv1

Please don't think of science as some sort of impossible mountain to climb. Yes there are some challenging bits but it's not as difficult as people think. Take your time, work hard and believe in yourself. When you find a topic difficult, don't give up. Just go to a different topic and come back to it later.

Finally, if you have any feedback on the workbooks, you're welcome to let me know (support@freesciencelessons.co.uk). I'm always keen to make the workbooks better so if you have a suggestion, I'd love to hear it.

Good luck on your journey. I hope that you get the grades that you want.

Shaun Donnelly

Shaun Donnelly

# Revision Tips

The first important point about revision is that you need to be realistic about the amount of work that you need to do. Essentially you have to learn two years of work (or three if you start GCSEs in Year 9). That's a lot of stuff to learn. So give yourself plenty of time. If you're very serious about getting a top grade then I would recommend starting your revision as early as you can. I see a lot of messages on Youtube and Twitter from students who leave their revision until the last minute. That's their choice but I don't think it's a good way to get the best grades.

To revise successfully for any subject (but I believe particularly for science), you have to really get into it. You have to get your mind deep into the subject. That's because science has some difficult concepts that require thought and concentration. So you're right in the middle of that challenging topic and your phone pings. Your friend has sent you a message about something that he saw on Netflix. You reply and start revising again. Another message appears. This is from a different friend who has a meme they want to share. And so on and so on.

What I'm trying to tell you is that successful revision requires isolation. You need to shut yourself away from distractions and that includes your phone. Nothing that any of your friends have to say is so critically important that it cannot wait until you have finished. Just because your friends are bored does not mean that your revision has to suffer. Again, it's about you taking control.

Remember to give yourself breaks every now and then. You'll know when it's time. I don't agree with people who say you need a break every fifteen minutes (or whatever). Everyone is different and you might find that your work is going so well that you don't need a break. In that case don't take one. If you're taking breaks every ten minutes then the question I would ask is do you need them? Or are you trying to avoid work?

There are many different ways to revise and you have to find what works for you. I believe that active revision is the most effective. I know that many students like to copy out detailed notes (often from my videos). Personally, I don't believe that this is a great way to revise since it's not really active. A better way is to watch a video and then try to answer the questions from this book. If you can't, then you might want to watch the video again (or look carefully at the answers to check the part that you struggled with).

The human brain learns by repetition. So the more times that you go over a concept, the more fixed it will become in your brain. That's why revision needs so much time because you really need to go over everything more than once (ideally several times) before the exam.

# Revision Tips

I find with my students that flashcards are a great way to learn facts. Again, that's because the brain learns by repetition. My students write a question on one side and the answer on the other. They then practise them until they've memorised the answer. I always advise them to start by memorising five cards and then gradually adding in extra cards, rather than try to memorise fifty cards at once.

I've noticed over the last few years that more students do past paper practise as a way of revising. I do not recommend this at all. A past paper is what you do AFTER you have revised. Imagine that you are trying to learn to play the guitar. So you buy a guitar and rather than having lessons, you book yourself into a concert hall to give a performance. And you keep giving performances until you can play. Would you recommend that as a good strategy? I wouldn't. But essentially that's how lots of students try to revise. Yes by all means do practise papers (I've included a specimen paper in this book for you) but do them at the end when you've done all your revision. Past papers require you to pull lots of different bits of the specification together, so you should only do them when you are capable of that (ie when you've already done loads of revision).

# A couple of final points ....

To reduce our environmental impact and to keep the price of this book reasonable, the answers are available online. Simply scan the QR code on the front or visit www.freesciencelessons.co.uk/b1cshv1

There will be times when I decide to update a book, for example to make something clearer or maybe to correct a problem (I hope not many of those). So please keep an eye out for updates. I'll post them on Twitter (@UKscienceguy) and also on the FAQ page of my website. If you think that you've spotted a mistake or a problem, please feel free to contact me.

# Contents


**Chapter 1: Cell Biology** .................... 8

Eukaryotes and Prokaryotes .................... 9

Sizes of Cells .................... 11

Order of Magnitude .................... 12

Animal Cells .................... 13

Plant Cells .................... 15

Animal Cell Specialisation .................... 17

Plant Cell Specialisation .................... 19

Required Practical: Microscopes .................... 21

Microscopy .................... 24

Cell Division by Mitosis .................... 26

Stem Cells .................... 28

Diffusion .................... 30

Surface Area to Volume Ratio .................... 32

Osmosis .................... 34

Required Practical: Effect of Osmosis on Plant Tissue .................... 36

Active Transport .................... 38

# Contents

**Chapter 2: Organisation** .................... 40

The Digestive System .................... 41

Digestive Enzymes .................... 44

Required Practical: Food Tests .................... 46

Effect of Temperature and pH on Enzymes .................... 48

Required Practical: Effect of pH on Amylase .................... 50

Absorption in the Small Intestine .................... 52

The Heart and Circulation .................... 53

Arteries, Veins and Capillaries .................... 55

The Blood .................... 56

Cardiovascular Diseases .................... 58

Gas Exchange in the Lungs .................... 60

Cancer .................... 61

Communicable and Non-communicable Diseases .................... 63

Correlating Risk Factors .................... 65

Lifestyle and Disease .................... 66

Plant Tissues .................... 67

Transpiration .................... 69

# Contents

**Chapter 3: Infection and Response** .................... 71

Communicable and Non-Communicable Diseases .................... 72

Pathogens .................... 74

Measles and HIV .................... 76

Salmonella and Gonorrhoea .................... 77

Malaria .................... 78

Non-specific Defence Systems .................... 79

The Immune System .................... 80

Infectious Diseases in Plants .................... 82

Vaccination .................... 83

Antibiotics .................... 85

Testing Medicines .................... 86

# Contents

**Chapter 4: Bioenergetics** .......... 88

Photosynthesis .......... 89

Uses of Glucose from Photosynthesis .......... 91

Required Practical: Photosynthesis .......... 92

Limiting Factors .......... 95

Respiration .......... 96

Exercise .......... 98

Metabolism .......... 99

# Chapter 1: Cell Biology

| |
|---|
| • Describe what is meant by a prokaryotic and eukaryotic cell and describe the features of these cells. |
| • Use common size units in standard and non-standard form and size prefixes (eg milli, micro, nano etc). |
| • Make order of magnitude calculations. |
| • Describe the main structures in animal cells and the functions of these structures. |
| • Describe the main structures in plant cells and the functions of these structures. |
| • Describe how different animal cells can be specialised to carry out their functions. |
| • Describe how different plant cells can be specialised to carry out their functions. |
| • Describe how to use a light microscope to view and draw plant and animal cells (required practical). |
| • Describe the advantages of electron microscopes over light microscopes. |
| • Make calculations involving magnification. |
| • Describe the process of cell division by mitosis and the role of cell division by mitosis in living organisms. |
| • Describe the features of stem cells (both embryonic and adult) and how stem cells can be used in medicine (including the role of embryonic cloning). |
| • Describe how particles can move by diffusion and describe the factors that affect the rate of diffusion. |
| • Calculate the surface area : volume ratio for an organism and explain how gills increase the surface area for diffusion of gases in fish. |
| • Describe what is meant by osmosis. |
| • Describe how to investigate the effects of osmosis on plant tissue (required practical). |
| • Describe how particles can move by active transport and describe the differences between active transport and diffusion. |

# Eukaryotes and Prokaryotes

**1.** Which of these is the correct definition of a eukaryotic cell?

- Eukaryotic cells have their cytoplasm enclosed in a cell membrane
- Eukaryotic cells contain their genetic material (DNA) enclosed in a nucleus
- Eukaryotic cells have their genetic material in the cytoplasm

**2.** The diagram below shows the structure of an animal cell. Animal cells are eukaryotic.

Draw a line from each label to the correct part of the cell.

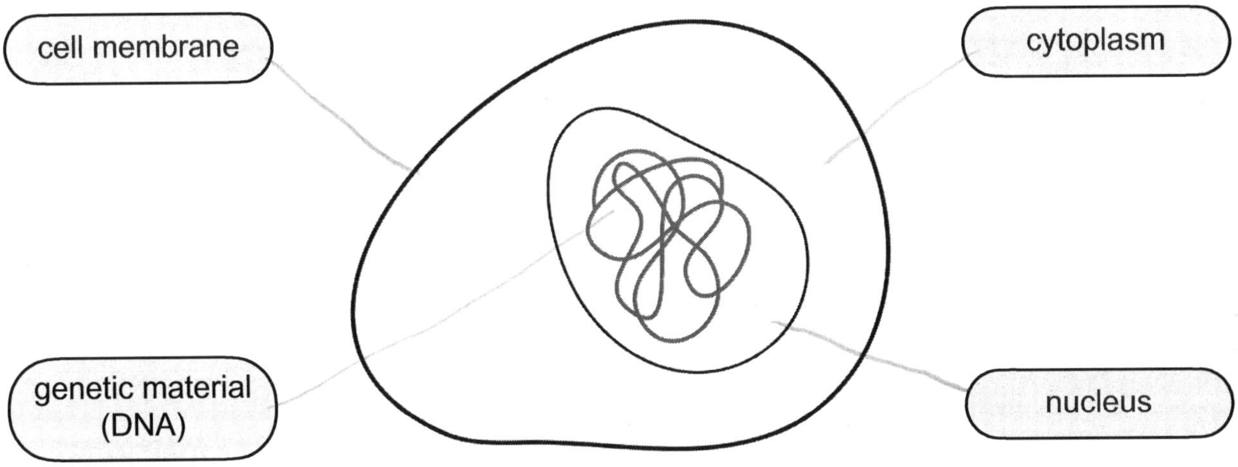


**3.** The statements below describe eukaryotic cells. Two of the statements are false.

Identify the false statements and write the correct versions below.

| Eukaryotic cells contain a cytoplasm | In eukaryotic cells, the cytoplasm is enclosed in a cell wall | In eukaryotic cells, the genetic material is found in the cytoplasm |
|---|---|---|
| True / False | True / False | True / False |

It is found in the nucleus

**4.** What is the definition of a prokaryotic cell?

Prokaryotic cells do contain their dna in the nucleus. enclosed

**5.** The diagram shows a bacterial cell. Bacteria are prokaryotic cells.

**a.** Label the diagram using the words below.

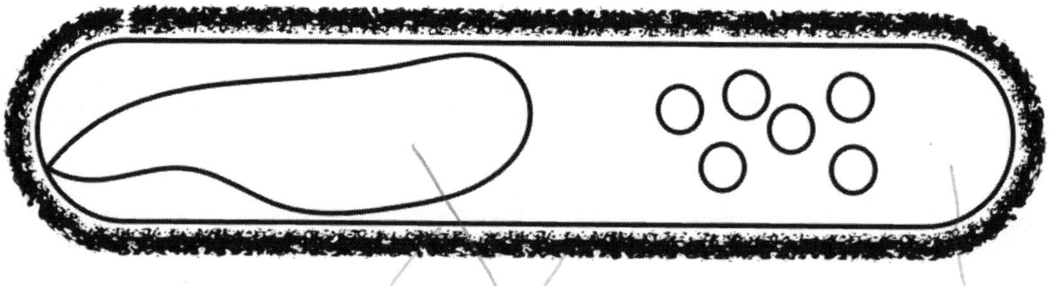

cell membrane | cell wall | loop of DNA | plasmids | cytoplasm

**b.** Label the parts of the diagram which show the genetic material of the prokaryotic cell.

**6.** Describe the two main differences between eukaryotic cells and prokaryotic cells.

| Location of genetic material | Sizes of the cells |
|---|---|
| enclosed in the nucleus<br>not, so it is DNA in form of plasmids | Prokaryotic cells are much smaller |

# Sizes of Cells

**1.** Complete the sentence by selecting the correct word from the list.

**centimetre** **nanometre** **metre** **millimetre**

All sizes in science are based on the ________________

**2.** The length of an insect such as a wasp is around 2 centimetres (cm).

**a.** How many centimetres are found in one metre (1 m)?

**b.** Which of the following shows the length of a wasp in standard form?

$2 \times 10^{-2}$ m

$1 \times 10^{-3}$ m

$2 \times 10^{-3}$ m

**3.** Millimetres are sometimes used to describe sizes in Biology.

**a.** The word "milli" means 1 / 1000th. How many millimetres are in 1 metre?

10

100

1000

**b.** What is 1 mm in standard form?

**4.** A very common unit in Biology is the micrometre (μm).

**a.** How many micrometres are in 1 metre?

**b.** Which of the following shows 6 μm in standard form?

$6 \times 10^{-10}$ m

$6 \times 10^{-9}$ m

$6 \times 10^{-6}$ m

**c.** What is the diameter of a typical human cell?

**5.** A nanometre (nm) is a tiny size and is sometimes used in Biology.

State how many nanometres are in 1 metre and express 1 nm in standard form.

Number of nanometres in 1 metre =

1 nanometre in standard form =

# Order of Magnitude

**1.** A cat and a small dog are around the same order of magnitude.

What is meant by the same order of magnitude?

**2.** A grapefruit has a diameter of around 15 cm and a grape has a diameter of around 1.5 cm.

Which of these best describes the relative sizes of a grapefruit and a grape?

| | | |
|---|---|---|
| The diameter of the grapefruit is around 1 order of magnitude smaller than the grape | The diameter of the grape is around 2 orders of magnitude smaller than the grapefruit | The diameter of the grapefruit is around 1 order of magnitude larger than the grape |

**3.** The length of an African elephant is around 7 m. The length of a mouse is around 7 cm.

Complete the sentences by selecting the correct words from the boxes.

The length of the mouse is around [ 0.7 / 0.07 / 0.007 ] metres. The elephant is [ 10 x / 100 x / 1000 x ] longer than the mouse.

This means that the elephant is [ 1 / 2 / 3 ] orders of magnitude longer than the mouse.

**4.** If we know how many times larger (or smaller) one object is compared to another, we can easily work out the order of magnitude difference.

Describe how we can do this.

**5.** Use a ruler to measure the length of the arrows below.

State how many orders of magnitude the bottom arrow is shorter than the top arrow.

# Animal Cells

**1.** Animal cells contain a number of different structures.

Complete the following paragraph using the words below.

**proteins** **cytoplasm** **eukaryotic** **mitochondria** **nucleus** **molecules**

Animal cells are ________________. This means that their genetic material (DNA) is enclosed in a ________________. The whole cell is enclosed within a cell membrane which controls which ________________ can enter and leave the cell. The ________________ is a watery solution where chemical reactions take place (for example the first stage of respiration). Animal cells also contain mitochondria and ribosomes. Aerobic respiration takes place in ________________ .

Ribosomes are where ________________ are synthesised.

**2.** Explain why ribosomes cannot be seen with a light microscope.

low resolution

**3.** The diagram below shows a general animal cell. Label the different structures in the cell.

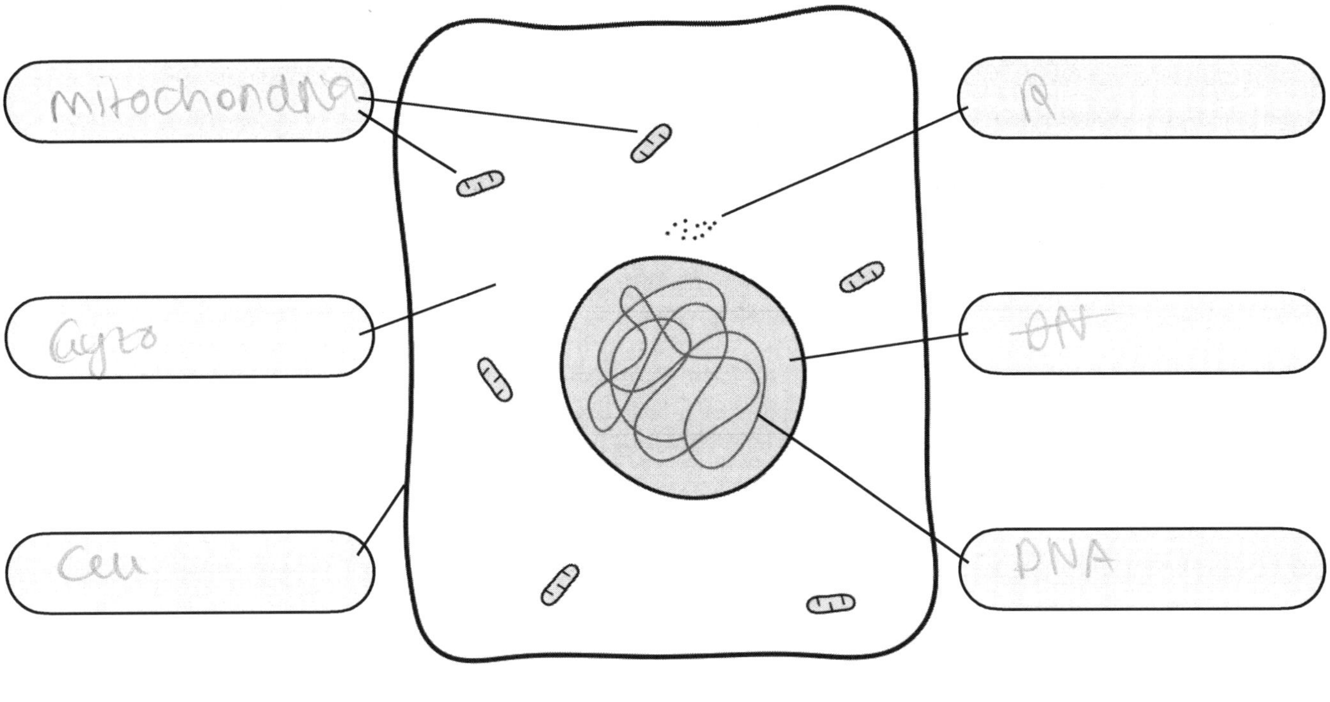

**4.** In the exam, you could be expected to compare the relative sizes of different parts of cells.

**a.** Use a ruler to measure the diameter of the nucleus in mm.

Diameter of nucleus = ________________________ mm

**b.** Now use a ruler to measure the length of a mitochondrion in mm.

Length of mitochondrion = _____________________ mm

**c.** How many times larger is the nucleus compared to a mitochondrion?

**d.** In an animal cell the diameter of the nucleus is around 10 μm.

Using your answer to question c, calculate the actual length of a mitochondrion in μm.

**e.** We can express the sizes of cells using standard form.

The size of the nucleus is given below. Write the size of the mitochondrion.

Size of nucleus = $1 \times 10^{-5}$ m

Size of mitochondrion = ...................... m

**5.** Draw a line from each part of a cell to the correct function.

| | |
|---|---|
| Nucleus | This controls the molecules that enter and leave the cell. |
| Cell membrane | These are where proteins are synthesised in the cell. |
| Cytoplasm | These are where aerobic respiration takes place in the cell. |
| Ribosomes | This is found in eukaryotic cells and contains the genetic material (DNA) of the cell. |
| Mitochondria | This is a watery solution where chemical reactions take place. |

# Plant Cells

**1.** Which of the following statements are correct?

| | | |
|---|---|---|
| Plant cells can easily change their shape | Animal cells can easily change their shape | A plant cell has a fixed shape which it cannot change |

**2.** The diagram below shows a plant cell that is found in leaves.

**a.** Label the diagram to show the different structures within the plant cell.

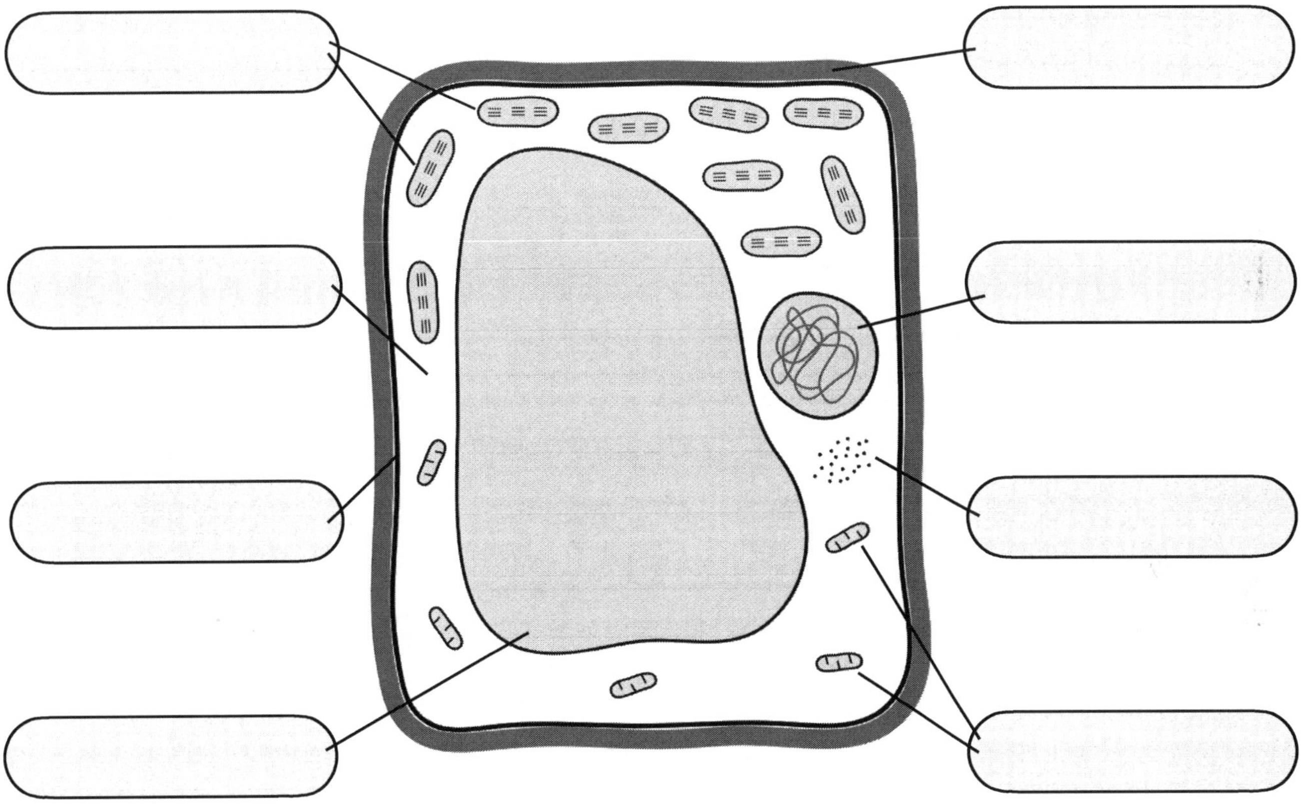

**b.** How does the diagram show that plant cells are eukaryotic?

**c.** Sunlight shines onto the top half of the cell. How is the structure of the plant cell adapted for this?

**3.** Tick the correct box to show whether each part of the cell is found in animal cells, plant cells or both.

| | Animal cells | Plant cells |
|---|---|---|
| Cell membrane | ☐ | ☐ |
| Vacuole | ☐ | ☐ |
| Cytoplasm | ☐ | ☐ |
| Chloroplasts | ☐ | ☐ |
| Mitochondria | ☐ | ☐ |
| Ribosomes | ☐ | ☐ |
| Cell wall | ☐ | ☐ |
| Nucleus | ☐ | ☐ |

**4.** Three important parts of a plant cell are the chloroplasts, the cell wall and the vacuole.

**a.** How are chloroplasts adapted to carry out photosynthesis?

**b.** What is the function of the plant cell wall?

**c.** What role does the vacuole play in the plant cell?

# Animal Cell Specialisation

Exam tip: Six mark questions do not have to be about required practicals. Adaptations of cells would make a great six mark question so don't be surprised to see it.

**1.** Complete the following paragraph using the words below.

**differentiation** **specialised** **function** **adaptations**

Most animal cells are ____________________ . This means that they have ____________________

which help them to carry out their ____________________ .

When cells become specialised, scientists call that ____________________ .

**2.** The diagram below shows the process of fertilisation.

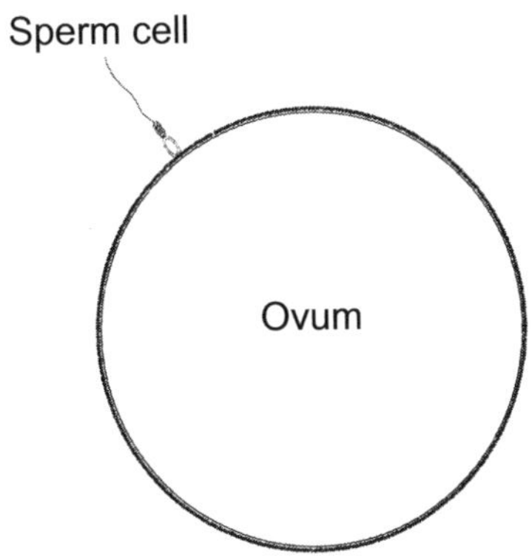


**a.** Describe what happens during fertilisation.

**b.** Both sperm cells and ovum cells only contain half of the genetic information found in normal adult cells.

Suggest the benefit of this.

**3.** The diagram below shows a sperm cell.

**a.** Label the diagram to show the nucleus, the mitochondria, the tail and enzymes.

**b.** Complete the table to show the purpose of each adaptation of the sperm cell.

| Adaptation | Purpose |
|---|---|
| Long tail | |
| Streamlined cell shape | |
| Lots of mitochondria | |
| Enzymes near nucleus | |

**4.** Another animal cell which is adapted for its function is the nerve cell (these are also called neurones).

**a.** What is the function of a nerve cell?

**b.** The diagram below shows the structure of a nerve cell.

Label the diagram to show the axon, myelin, synapses and dendrites.

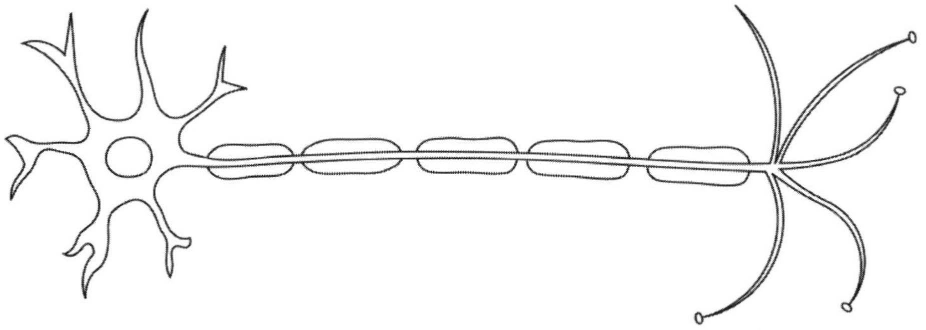

**c.** Draw a line to link each adaptation to the correct function.

| | |
|---|---|
| Axon | These are junctions which allow one nerve cell to pass impulses to other nerve cells |
| Myelin | This long structure carries electrical impulses from the nerve cell body down to the synapses |
| Synapses | These increase the surface area, allowing other nerve cells to connect more easily |
| Dendrites | This is an insulating material which helps to speed up the transmission of the electrical impulses |

**5.** Muscle cells are adapted so that they can contract (get shorter). This is shown in the diagram.

**a.** How are muscle cells adapted to contract?

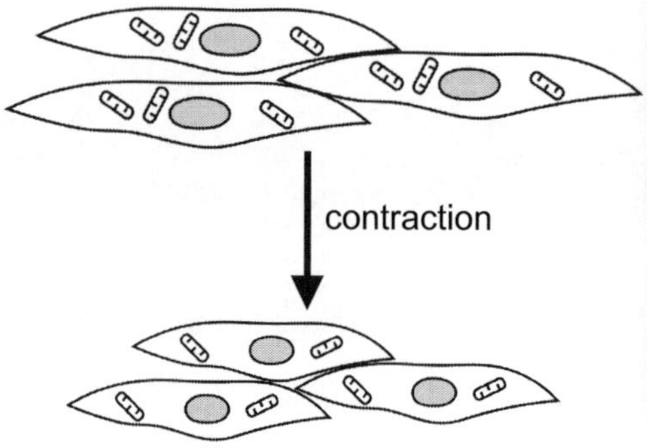


**b.** Contraction requires a lot of energy. How are muscle cells adapted to provide this?

**c.** What do scientists call muscle cells working together?

# Plant Cell Specialisation

1. The structures found in eukaryotic cells are listed below.

Circle the structures that are found only in plant cells.

| | | | |
|---|---|---|---|
| Cell membrane | Vacuole | Cytoplasm | Chloroplasts |
| Mitochondria | Ribosomes | Cell wall | Nucleus |

2. Root hair cells are found in the roots of plants.

a. State the function of a root hair cell.

b. A diagram of a root hair cell is shown below.

Label the diagram to show the structures found in a root hair cell.

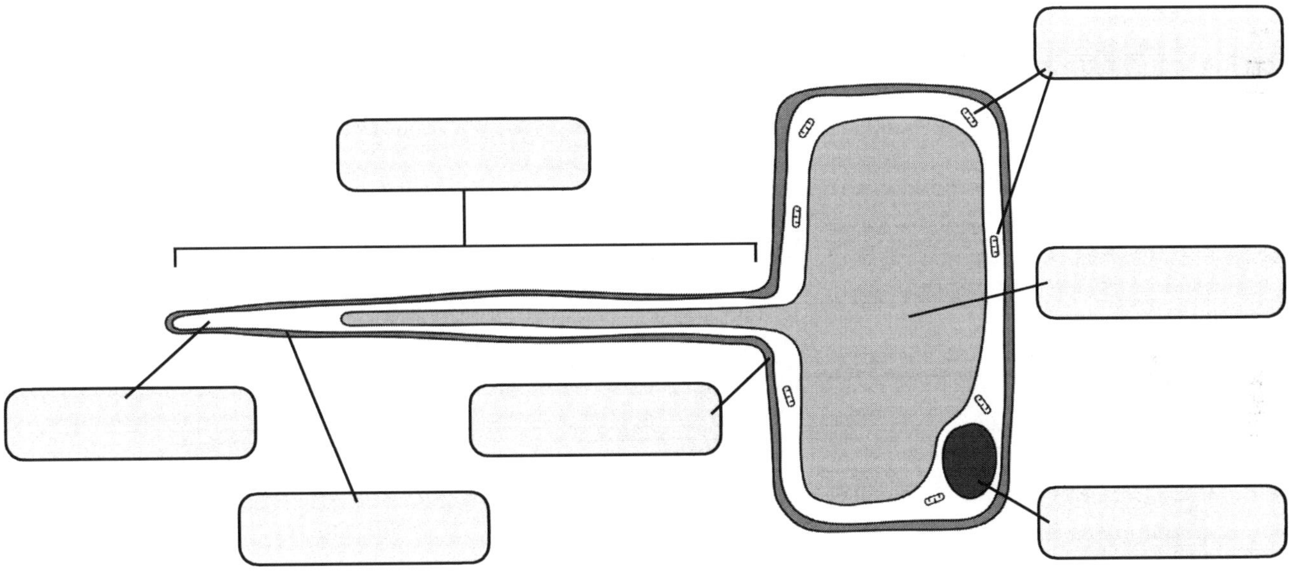

c. Explain how the root hair allows the cell to carry out its function.

d. Why do root hair cells not contain any chloroplasts?

**3.** Another type of specialised plant cell is found in the xylem. Xylem form hollow tubes running through the stem of a plant.

**a.** Describe the function of xylem.

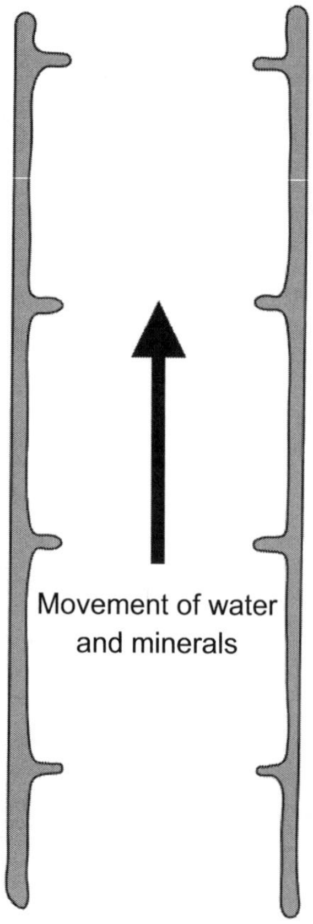


**b.** The diagram shows a xylem vessel.

Label the diagram to show the thick walls containing lignin and the remains of end walls.

**c.** Complete the table to show the purpose of the different adaptations found in xylem.

| Adaptation | Purpose |
|---|---|
| Thick walls containing lignin | |
| No end walls between the cells | |
| No internal structures eg nucleus | |

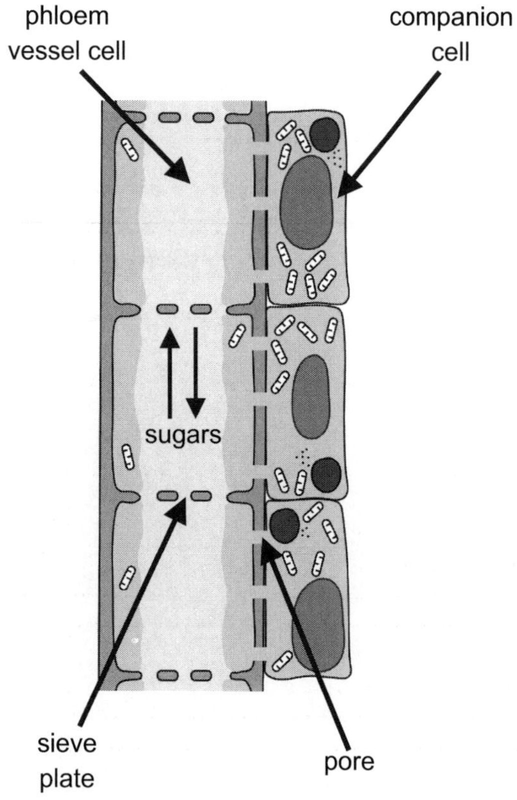


**4.** Phloem tubes are also found in the stem of plants. The diagram shows part of a phloem tube.

**a.** What is the function of phloem tubes?

**b.** How are the phloem vessel cells adapted to carry out this function?

**c.** What is the role of the companion cells?

# Required Practical: Microscopes

**1.** The diagram shows a light microscope such as the type used in schools in the UK.

**a.** Label the diagram using the labels at the bottom.

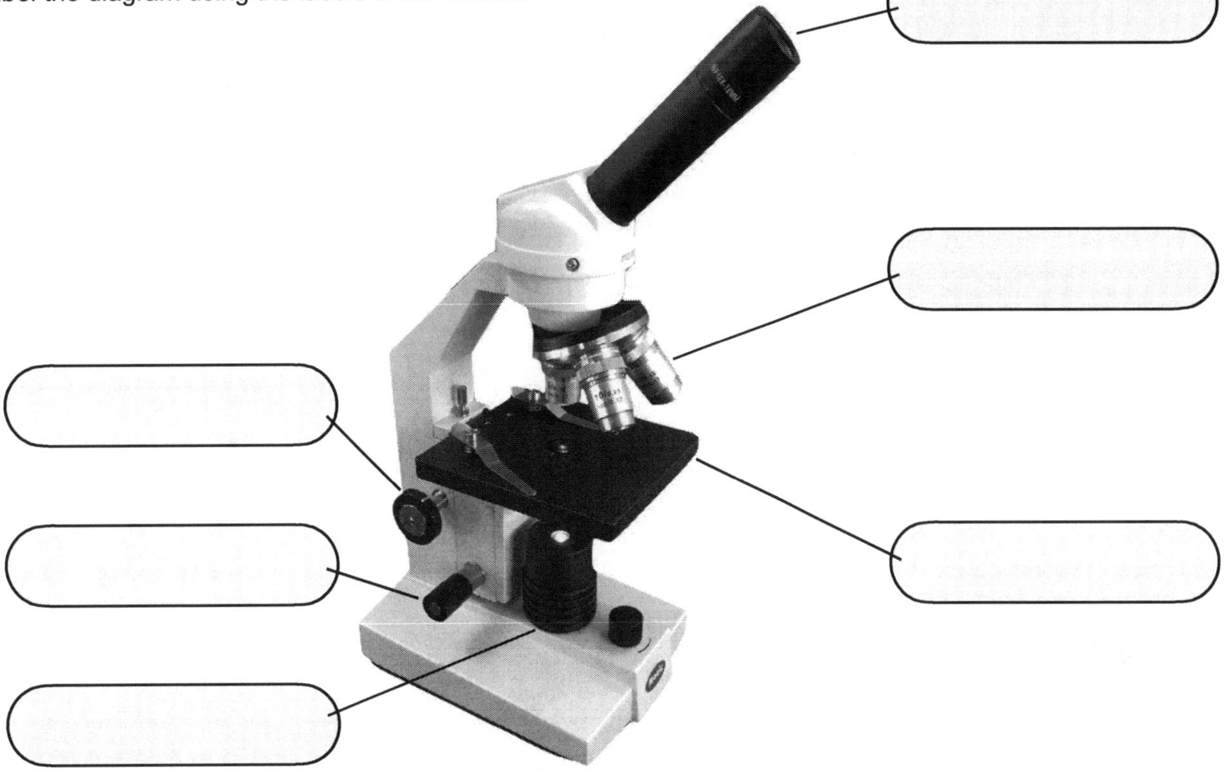

**objective lenses** | **stage** | **lamp** | **coarse focussing dial** | **eyepiece** | **fine focussing dial**

**b.** Draw a line to link the correct feature to the correct function.

| | |
|---|---|
| stage | These magnify the image. In school light microscopes, these have a magnification of 4x, 10x and 40x |
| lamp | This is where we view through. The eyepiece lens has a magnification of 10x |
| objective lenses | This allows us to rapidly move the stage towards and away from the objective lens, focusing the image |
| eyepiece | This is where we place the microscope slide that we want to view |
| coarse focussing dial | This is used to move the stage up or down by a very small amount, allowing us to focus on fine detail |
| fine focussing dial | This provides illumination. Light from this shines through the specimen and into the objective lens |

**2.** In the exam, you could be asked to describe the stages of using a light microscope to view a prepared slide.

**a.** First we place the slide on the stage and secure it with the clips.

Explain the purpose of using the clips.

**b.** We then adjust the objective lens to the lowest power.

Which is the lowest power objective lens?

| 4x | 10x | 40x |
|---|---|---|

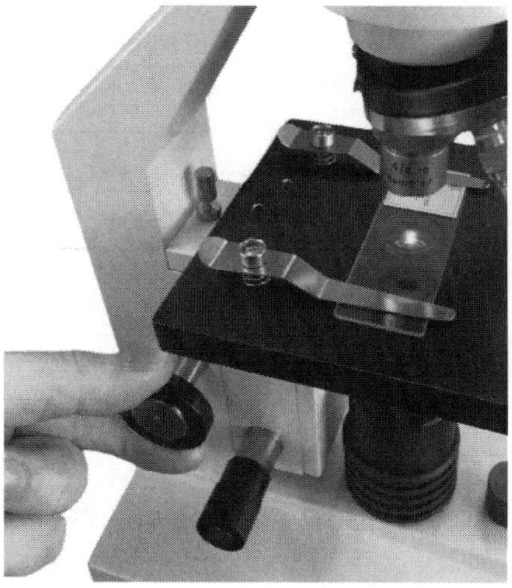

**c.** We now use the coarse focussing dial so that the objective lens is almost touching the microscope slide.

While we do this, it is very important that we look at the microscope from the side rather than through the eyepiece.

Suggest a reason why we need to look from the side rather than through the eyepiece.

**d.** When the objective lens is almost touching the slide, we can look down the eyepiece and use the fine focussing dial until the cells come into focus.

Describe the role of the fine focussing dial at this point.

**e.** A student set the objective lens to x10. Calculate the total magnification provided by the microscope.

3. Using a light microscope in a school, we can see certain structures in animal cells.

a. Complete the table to show what we can see.

| Structure | Can clearly be seen with a light microscope | Can sometimes be seen with a light microscope | Too small to be seen with a light microscope |
|---|---|---|---|
| Nucleus | | | |
| Cell membrane | | | |
| Cytoplasm | | | |
| Mitochondria | | | |
| Ribosome | | | |

**b.** List the structures that may be seen when viewing a plant cell with a light microscope in a school.

**c.** Once we have drawn our pencil diagram of the cells we are viewing, we need to add a scale bar. Describe how we produce a scale bar.

**d.** The picture below shows onion cells seen through a light microscope.

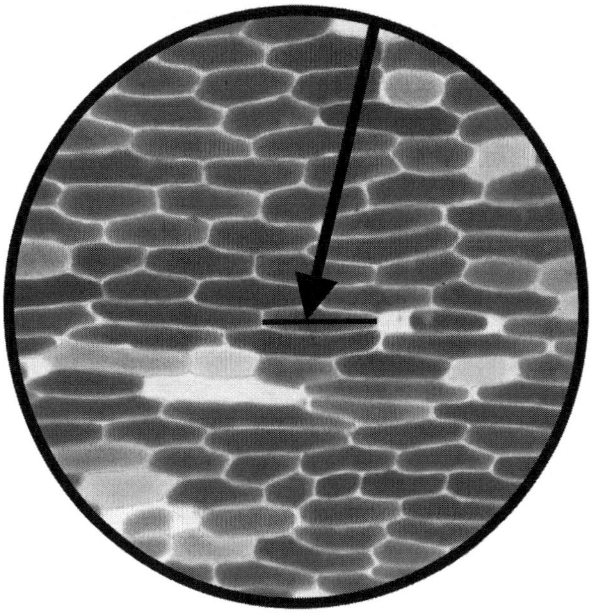

The arrow points to a single onion cell. Use a ruler to measure the length of the cell (in mm).

The approximate length of an onion cell is 0.1 mm. Determine the magnification of the image above.

# Microscopy

**1.** Complete the following paragraph using the words below.

**small** **resolution** **detail** **magnify** **magnification**

Light microscopes allow us to _______________. This means that the image is much larger than the object we are looking at. Light microscopes have two main disadvantages. Firstly, they have a limited _______________ This means that they cannot view very_______________ structures inside a cell. Secondly, light microscopes have a limited _________________. Because of this, images can appear blurred and we cannot make out fine _________________ .

**2.** Explain why electron microscopes are more useful than light microscopes for viewing details inside cells.

**3.** If we are shown an image from a microscope, we can calculate the magnification. To do that, we use the triangle on the right.

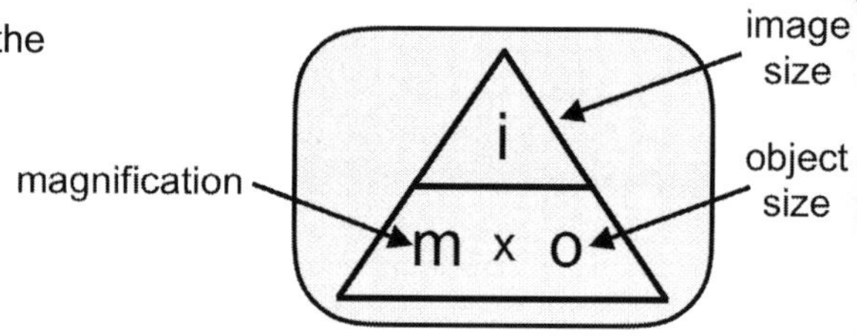


**a.** The diagram below shows a muscle cell.

Use a ruler to measure the length (in mm) of the nucleus shown.

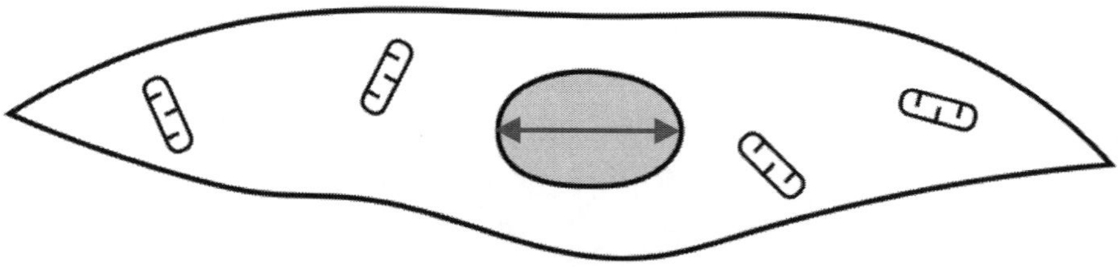

**b.** The actual length of the nucleus is 0.01 mm. Determine the magnification.

Exam tip: In the exam, you could be asked to convert sizes from millimetres (mm) to micrometres (μm). Remember that 1 millimetre = 1000 micrometres.

**4.** The diagram below shows a sperm cell.

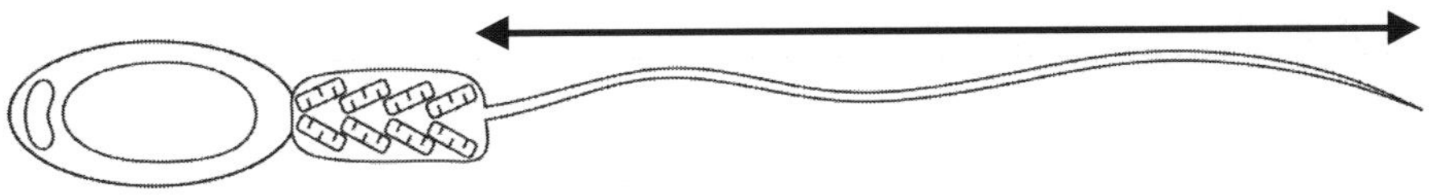

**a.** Use a ruler to measure the length of the tail in millimetres (mm).

Length of tail = ________________ mm

**b.** Convert the length of the tail to micrometres (μm).

Length of tail = ________________ μm

**c.** The actual length of the sperm tail is 50 μm. Determine the magnification.

**5.** The diagram below shows a number of mitochondria.

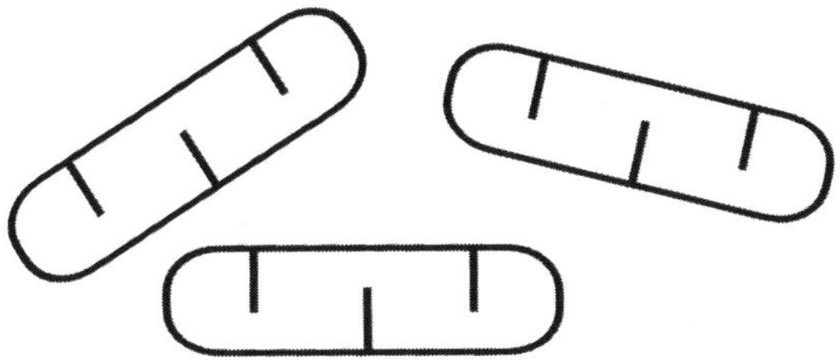

**a.** Use a ruler to measure the length of a mitochondrion in mm.

Length of mitochondrion = ________________ mm

**b.** Convert the length of the mitochondrion to micrometres (μm).

Length of mitochondrion = ________________ μm

**c.** The magnification of the diagram is 17 000x.

Determine the actual length of the mitochondrion in micrometres (μm).

Actual length of mitochondrion = ________________ μm

# Cell Division by Mitosis

**1.** The diagram below shows an animal cell (this is not from a human).

**a.** Label the diagram with the names of the structures shown.

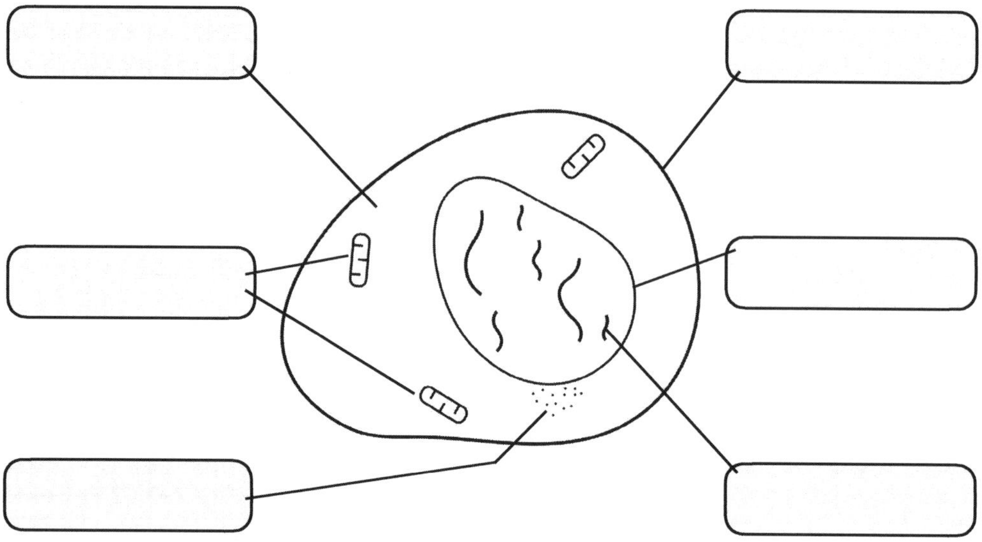

**b.** Complete the sentences by selecting the correct words from the boxes.

In the nucleus of cells, we find [mitochondria / ribosomes / chromosomes]. These are made of the molecule [RNA / DNA / enzymes].

The cell in the diagram contains [6 / 4 / 2] chromosomes. In body cells, chromosomes are [single / pairs / triples].

Human body cells contain [23 pairs of / 46 pairs of / 23 single] chromosomes.

**c.** Label the chromosome pairs in the diagram above.

**d.** Name the type of cell where chromosomes are not paired.

**e.** Explain how chromosomes determine our inherited features.

**2.** When cells divide, scientists call this the cell cycle.

The cell cycle including mitosis is shown below.

Describe what is happening in each stage.

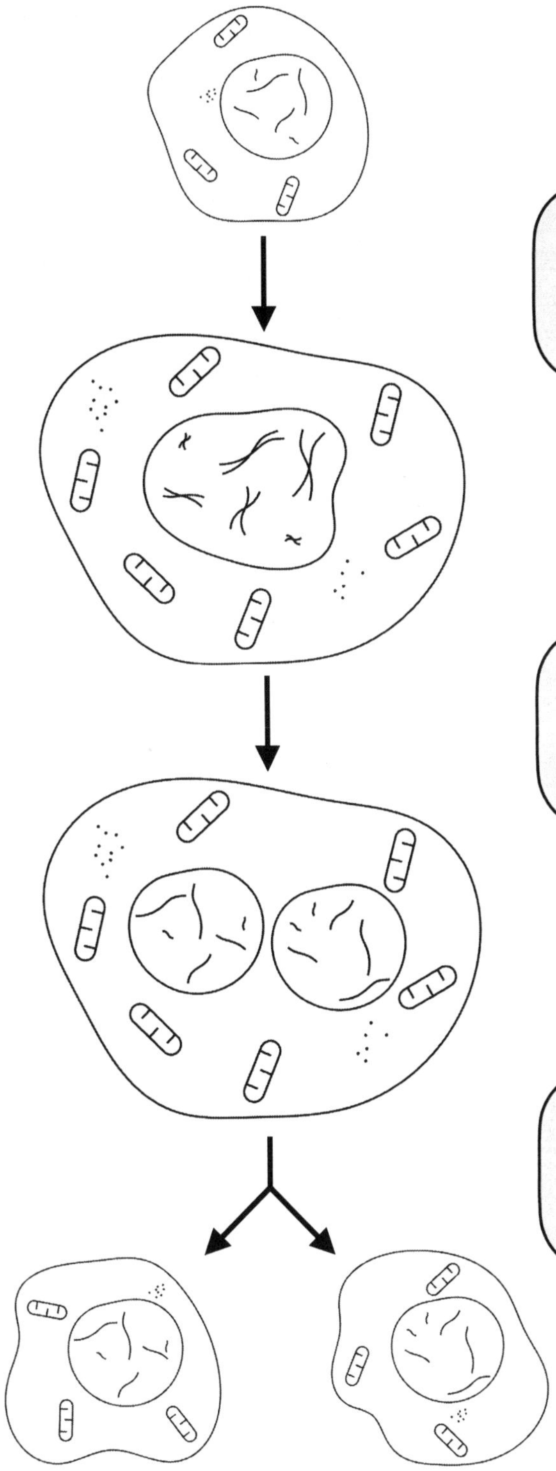

Stage 1:

Stage 2:

Stage 3:

**3.** Describe three functions of cell division by mitosis.

# Stem Cells

**1.** The stages leading to the formation of an adult human are shown below.

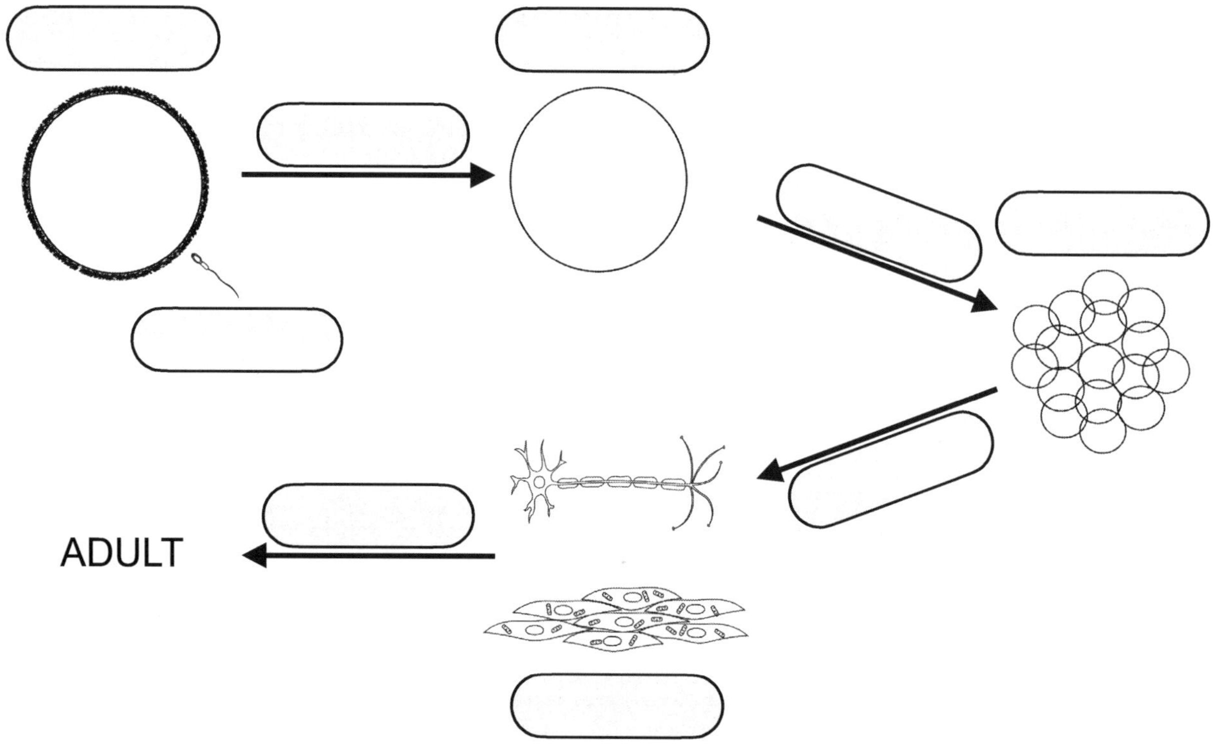


**a.** Label the diagram using the labels below.

specialised cells | mitosis | ovum | fertilised ovum | differentiation

sperm | fertilisation | embryo | mitosis

**b.** Cells in the embryo are called embryonic stem cells.

What is meant by a stem cell?

**c.** As well as in an embryo, we can also find stem cells in adults, for example in the bone marrow.

How are stem cells in the bone marrow different from stem cells in the embryo (tick the correct box)?

- Stem cells in the embryo are smaller than stem cells in bone marrow ☐
- Bone marrow stem cells only differentiate to form a small number of cell types ☐
- Bone marrow stem cells cannot undergo cell division by mitosis ☐

**d.** Which type of cells are produced from bone marrow stem cells?

2. Stem cells have several uses in medicine. One use is in a bone marrow transplant.

Complete the following paragraph using the words below.

**compatible donor radiation transplant mitosis viruses differentiating leukaemia**

Cancer of the bone marrow is called ____________________ . This is treated with a bone marrow ____________________ First, ____________________ is used to destroy the patient's existing bone marrow. Bone marrow from a live ____________________ is then transplanted into the patient. The donated stem cells now undergo ____________________ , forming new bone marrow as well as ____________________ to form new blood cells. We need to use a ____________________ donor to prevent the white blood cells from attacking the patient's body. Donated bone marrow also carries the risk of infecting the patient with ____________________ .

3. Stem cells can also be produced by therapeutic cloning.

In therapeutic cloning, an embryo is produced with the same genes as the patient. Stem cells from the embryo are then transplanted into the patient.

**a.** Describe the advantage of using stem cells produced by therapeutic cloning compared with donated stem cells.

**b.** Stem cells produced by therapeutic cloning could be used to treat diabetes or paralysis. However, some people object to using stem cells produced by therapeutic cloning.

Suggest why some people object to using stem cells produced by therapeutic cloning?

4. Plant cells also contain stem cells. These are found in meristem tissue at the roots and the buds.

**a.** State one way that plant stem cells from meristem tissue are different from adult cell stem cells in humans.

**b.** Describe two uses of plant meristem tissue.

# Diffusion

Exam tip: The definition of diffusion is a very common exam question and students often lose marks on this. I'd recommend that you learn the definition.

**1.** Many molecules move in and out of cells by diffusion.

**a.** Complete the sentences by selecting the correct words from the boxes.

Diffusion is the spreading out of particles resulting in a net movement from an area of [lower concentration / higher concentration / equal concentration]

to an area of [lower concentration. / higher concentration. / equal concentration.]

**b.** What is meant by "net movement"?

**c.** The diagrams below show three cells. The black dots represent molecules.

In each case, state the direction of net movement and explain your answer.

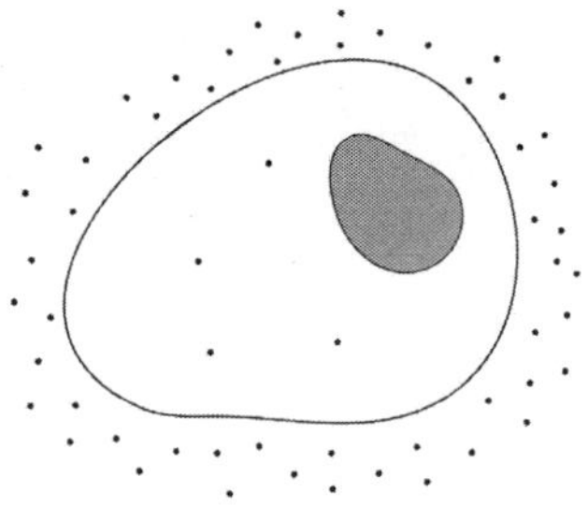

Net movement = In / Out / Neither

Explanation

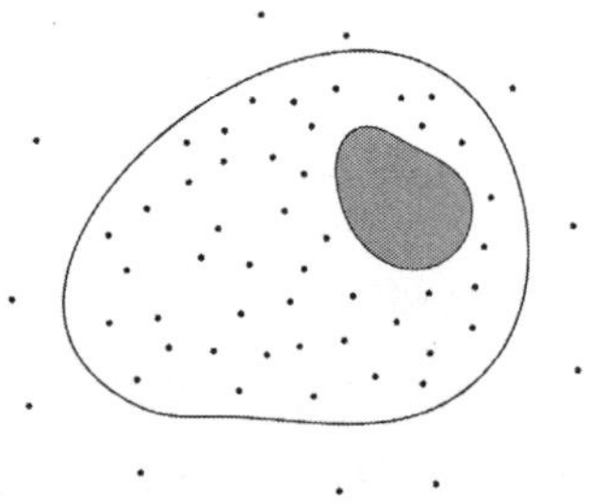

Net movement = In / Out / Neither

Explanation

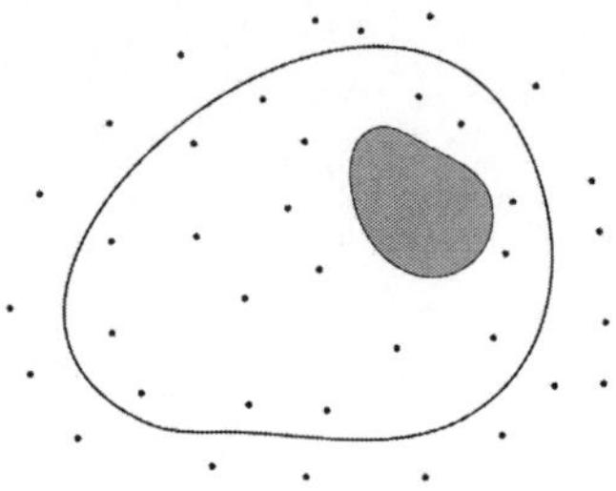

Net movement = In / Out / Neither

Explanation

**2.** The diagram below shows the levels of oxygen and carbon dioxide inside a muscle cell.

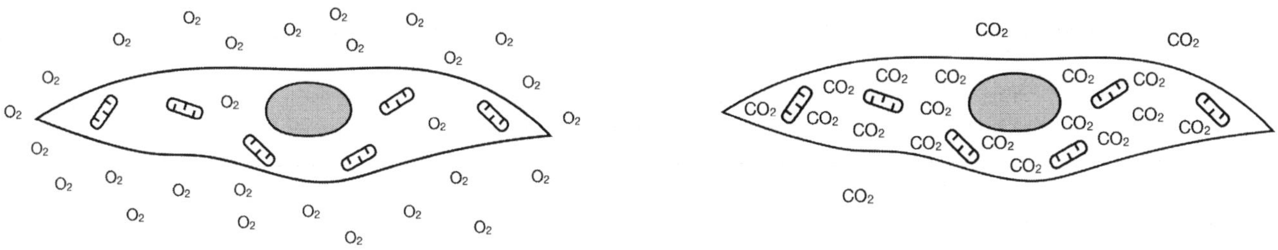


**a.** Explain why the concentration of oxygen is greater outside the cell and the concentration of carbon dioxide is greater inside the cell.

**b.** Draw arrows on the diagrams to show the diffusion of oxygen and carbon dioxide.

**c.** Urea is a waste product produced inside cells. Describe what happens to the urea produced by cells.

**3.** The rate of diffusion depends on three main factors.

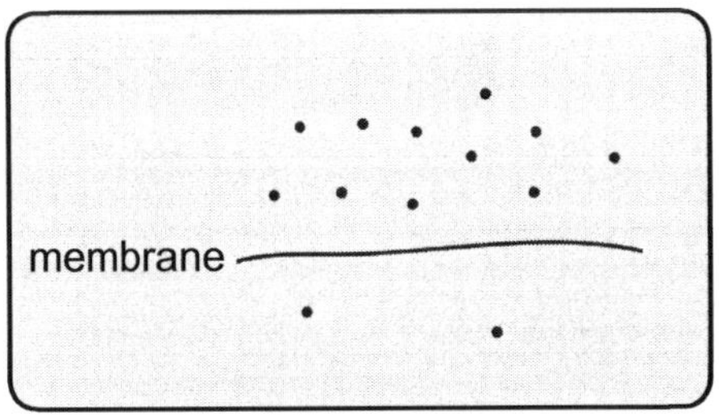


**a.** Diffusion is faster if the concentration gradient is greater.

What is meant by the concentration gradient?

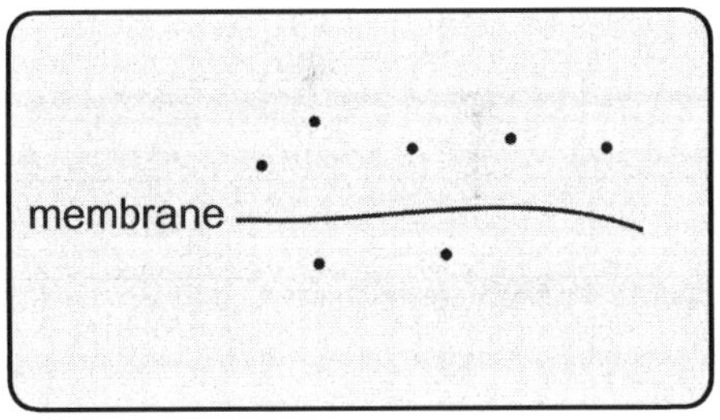


**b.** The diagrams show molecules on either side of a cell membrane.

Draw arrows on the diagrams to show how the rate of diffusion is different in each case and explain your answer.

**c.** The rate of diffusion increases at higher temperatures. Explain why.

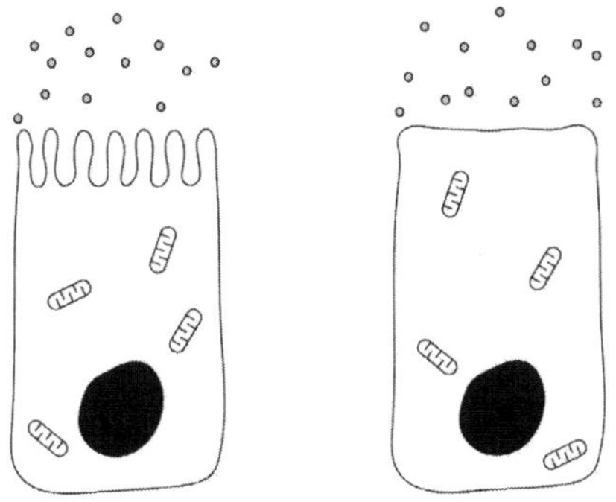

**Cell A** **Cell B**

**d.** The diagram shows two different types of cells.

In which cell will the rate of diffusion be greater? Explain your answer.

# Surface Area to Volume Ratio

Exam tip: As we saw in the last section, a greater surface area increases the rate of diffusion. You need to be able to describe different examples of this.

**1.** The surface area : volume ratio determines how easily oxygen gas can diffuse into an organism.

**a.** Which of the following is true about amoeba?

- Amoeba have a small surface area : volume ratio
- Amoeba can rely on diffusion to transport molecules in and out of the cell
- Amoeba are multicellular organisms
- Amoeba are single-celled organisms
- Amoeba have a large surface area : volume ratio
- Amoeba need gills to get oxygen in and out of the blood

**b.** The diagram below shows three organisms which are each cube-shaped.

For each organism, use a ruler to measure the length of the side. Assume that all the sides are the same length.

**Organism A**

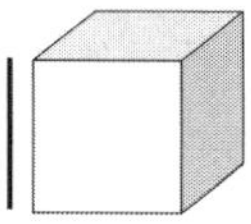

Length of side = ________________

Surface area = ________________

Volume = ________________

Surface area : volume ratio = ________________

**Organism B**

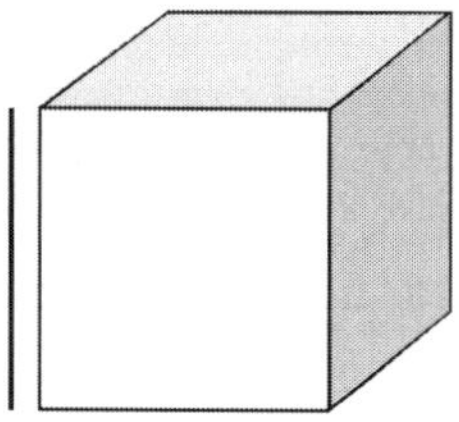

Length of side = ________________

Surface area = ________________

Volume = ________________

Surface area : volume ratio = ________________

**Organism C**

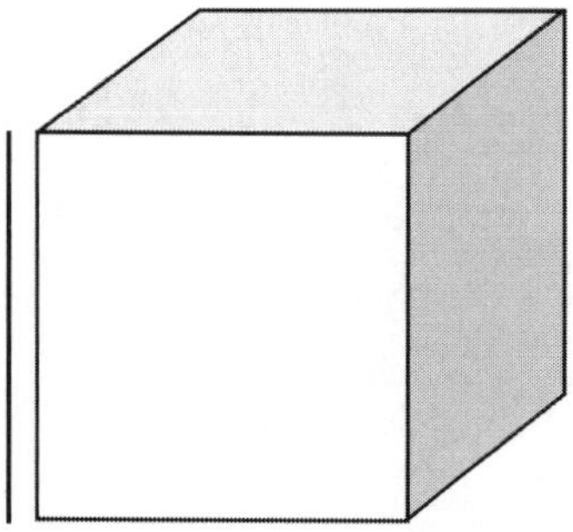

Length of side = ________________

Surface area = ________________

Volume = ________________

Surface area : volume ratio = ________________

**c.** What happens to the surface area : volume ratio as organisms get larger?

2. Multicellular organisms cannot rely on diffusion to provide all of their cells with oxygen.

a. What is meant by a multicellular organism?

b. Use the idea of surface area : volume ratio to explain why multicellular organisms cannot rely just on diffusion.

c. Describe two ways that multicellular organisms solve the problem of getting oxygen to their cells.

3. Fish are multicellular organisms which have solved the problem of getting oxygen to their cells.

a. Complete the following paragraph using the words below.

**blood** **filaments** **oxygen** **gills**

Fish take water into their mouth. This water contains dissolved ____________________ . The water then passes through the ____________________ where the oxygen diffuses into the bloodstream. The gills are covered with a large number of fine ____________________ where gases can pass in and out of the ____________________ .

b. The diagram below shows a filament in the gills of a fish.

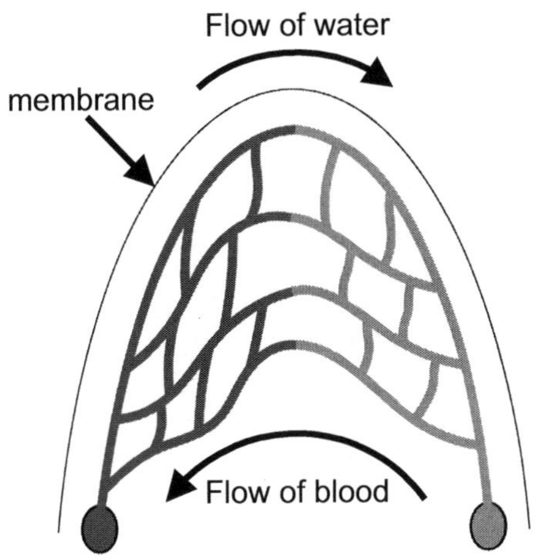


- Label the oxygenated blood (blood containing oxygen).
- Label the deoxygenated blood (blood containing no oxygen).
- Draw an arrow to show the diffusion of oxygen gas.

c. Describe three ways in which the filaments increase the rate of diffusion.

 

# Osmosis

Exam tip: Just like with diffusion, osmosis is a very common exam topic. It's critical that you learn the definition of osmosis and be prepared to state it in the exam.

**1.** The diagrams below show a dilute solution and a concentrated solution. Both solutions contain the same volume.

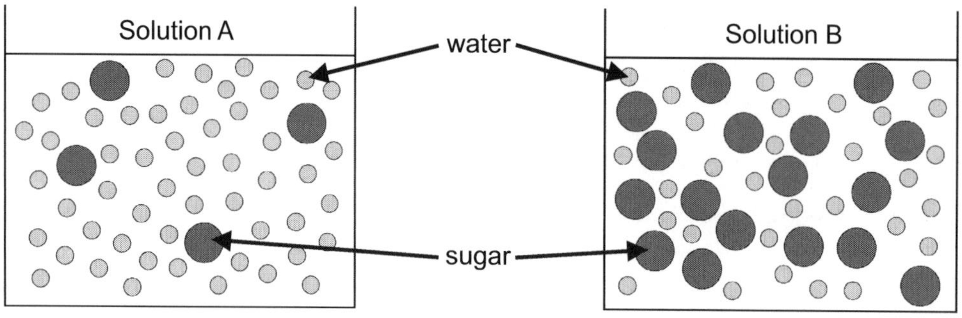


**a.** Solution B is a more concentrated sugar solution than solution A.

Explain why in terms of the number of water molecules.

**b.** In the diagram below, the solutions have been separated by a partially permeable membrane.

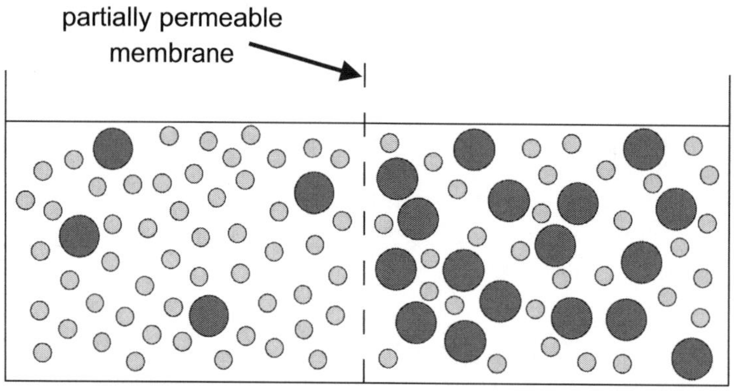


What is meant by a partially permeable membrane?

**c.** In the solutions above, osmosis will take place. Draw an arrow to show the direction of osmosis

**d.** Explain your answer to question c. In your answer you should include the definition of osmosis.

**2.** Osmosis can have large effects on animal and plant cells.

**a.** Which of the following is correct (circle one box)?

| | | |
|---|---|---|
| The cytoplasm of cells contains a large amount of water | The cytoplasm of cells contains virtually no water | The cytoplasm of cells contains a small amount of water |

**b.** The diagrams below show an animal cell placed in a more dilute solution and a more concentrated solution.

In both cases, draw what the cell would look like after osmosis has taken place and explain your answer.

**More dilute solution**

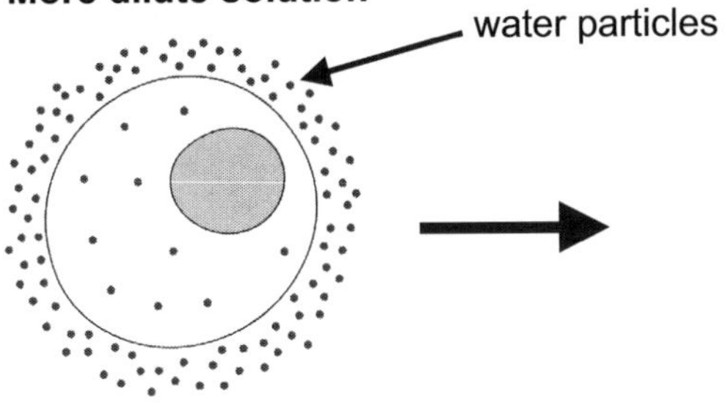


Explanation

**More concentrated solution**

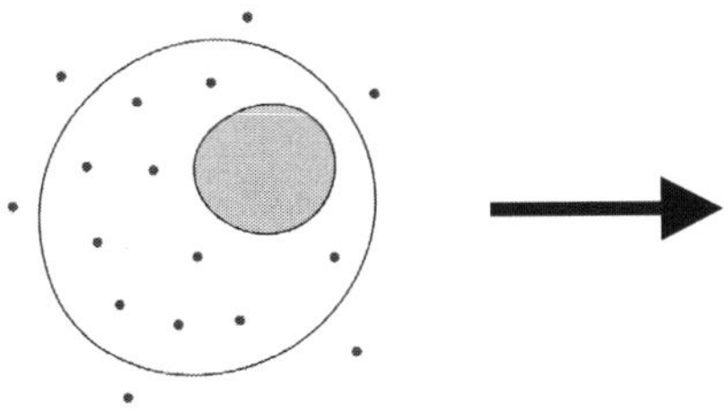

Explanation

**c.** Osmosis can also have large effects on plant cells.

The diagram shows a plant cell placed in a more dilute solution and in a more concentrated solution.

Complete the diagrams to show whether the cell becomes turgid or flaccid in the different solutions.

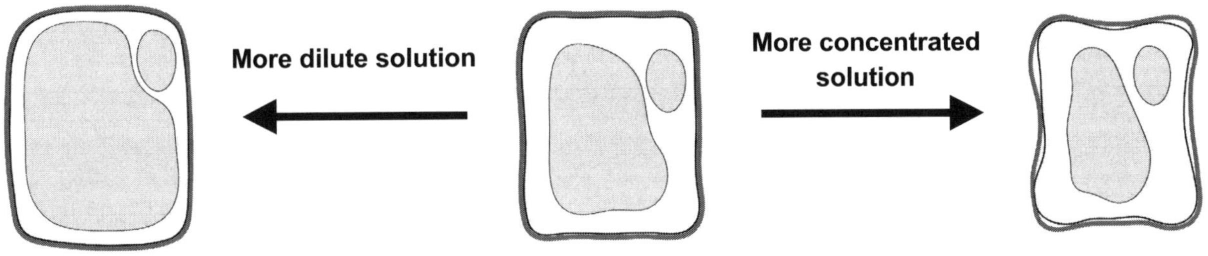


| | | |
|---|---|---|
| Plant cell swells and becomes turgid / flaccid | Normal plant cell | Plant cell shrinks and becomes turgid / flaccid |

**d.** Explain why the plant cell swells or shrinks in different concentrations.

**e.** Why does the plant cell not burst in very dilute solutions?

# Required Practical: Effect of Osmosis on Plant Tissue

Exam tip: Like all required practicals, try to get an overall idea of the equipment and method. Do not get hung up on exact measurements or quantities.

**1.** In this practical we are looking at the effect of osmosis on potato cells. Any other root vegetable also works well.

**a.** We start by peeling the potato. Explain why we need to remove the potato skin.

**b.** We then use a cork-borer to produce cylinders of potato.

Explain the advantage of using a cork-borer.

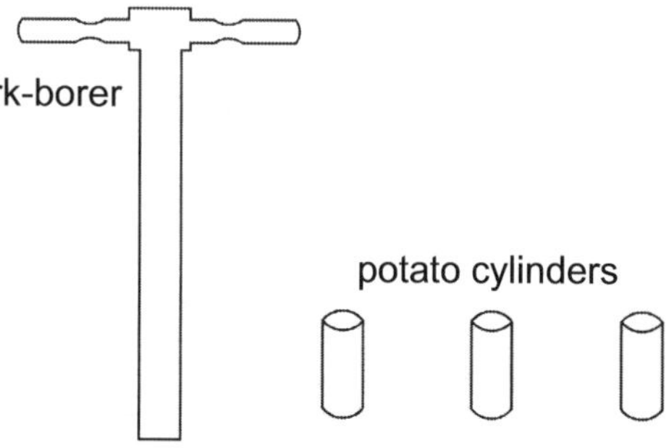


**c.** We then use a scalpel to cut all of the potato cylinders to the same length (eg 3 cm).

Why is it important that the cylinders are not too short?

**d.** Both the diameter and length of the cylinders are examples of (circle the correct answer):

Independent variables | Control variables | Dependent variables

**2.** Next we measure the mass and the length of the potato cylinders.

The resolution of a measuring instrument is the smallest value that can be measured. State the resolution of the balance on the right.

**3.** We now place the cylinders in different concentrations of sugar solution and leave overnight.

What do you think is the advantage of leaving the cylinders overnight rather than for an hour?

**4.** Lastly, we gently roll the cylinders on paper towel and then weigh them again and measure their length again.

Why is it important that we do not press on the potato cylinders?

**5.** Once we have weighed and measured the potato cylinders, we need to calculate the percentage change.

**a.** Calculate the percentage mass change of the potato cylinders shown.

Remember to include a positive (+) sign if the cylinder gained mass and a negative (-) sign if they lost mass.

| Potato cylinder 1 | | Potato cylinder 2 | |
|---|---|---|---|
| Start mass (g) | 2.75 | Start mass (g) | 2.78 |
| Mass gained (g) | 0.35 | Mass lost (g) | 0.64 |
| % change in mass | | % change in mass | |

| Potato cylinder 3 | | Potato cylinder 4 | |
|---|---|---|---|
| Start mass (g) | 2.82 | Start mass (g) | 2.73 |
| Final mass (g) | 2.26 | Final mass (g) | 3.40 |
| % change in mass | | % change in mass | |

**b.** What is the advantage of looking at percentage change in mass rather than simply mass?

**c.** We now plot the % changes in mass against the concentration of sugar.

This is shown in the graph below.

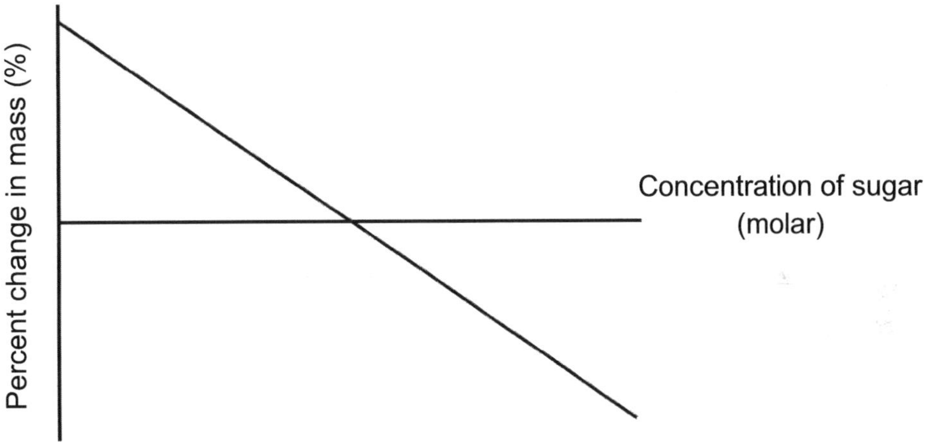


Label the graph to show:

- Where water has moved into the potato cylinders by osmosis.
- Where water has moved out of the potato cylinders by osmosis.

**d.** Label the graph to show where the concentration of the sugar solution is the same as the concentration of the potato cylinder.

Explain your answer.

**e.** Look again at your answers to question 5a.

Place a point on the line on the graph which approximately applies to each of the four potato cylinders.

# Active Transport

**1.** The diagrams below show particles on either side of a cell membrane.

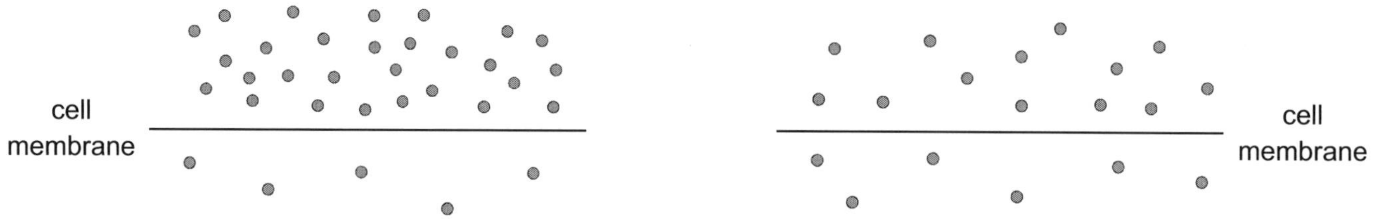


**a.** Both of the diagrams show a concentration gradient.

What is meant by a concentration gradient?

**b.** Draw an arrow on both diagrams to show the size of the concentration gradients.

**c.** In which of the two cells will diffusion be faster? Explain your answer.

**2.** Active transport is also used by cells to bring molecules into the cell.

**a.** What is the definition of active transport?

**b.** The diagram below shows particles moving into a cell. The arrow shows the direction of movement.

Draw an arrow on the diagram to show the direction of the concentration gradient.

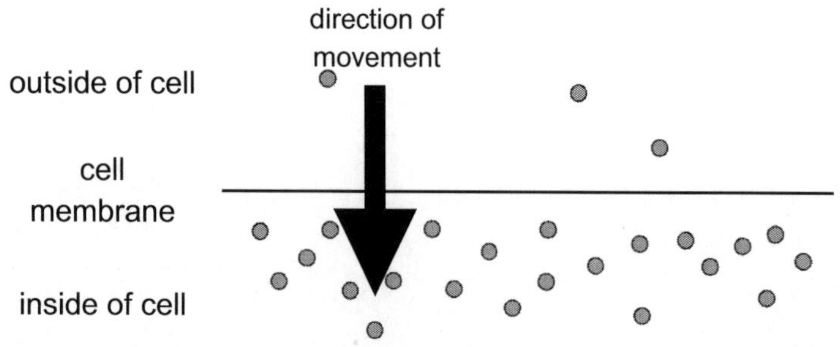


**c.** Explain how the diagram shows active transport.

3. Complete the following boxes to show the differences between diffusion and active transport.

| DIFFUSION | ACTIVE TRANSPORT |
| --- | --- |
| Particles move down / against the concentration gradient | Particles move down / against the concentration gradient |
| Does / does not require energy from respiration | Does / does not require energy from respiration |

4. Active transport takes place in many animal cells.

The diagram below shows a cell which lines the interior of the small intestine.

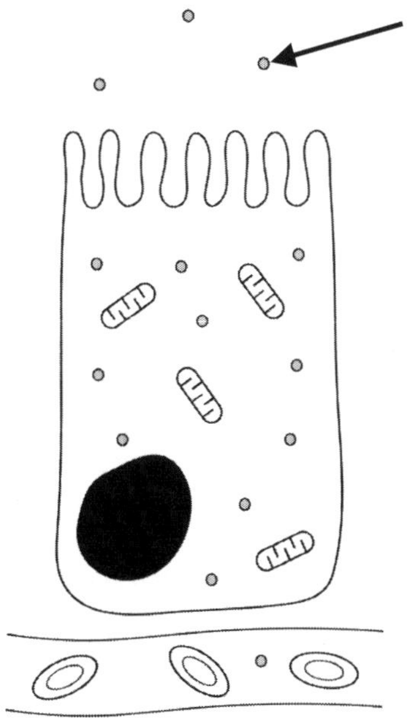


**a.** Draw an arrow to show the direction that sugar molecules such as glucose move by active transport.

**b.** Explain why glucose cannot move into the cell by diffusion.

**c.** Explain why the cells lining the small intestine contain a large number of mitochondria.

5. Active transport also takes place in plant cells.

The diagram shows a root hair cell. We saw these in the topic on specialised plant cells.

**a.** Root hair cells absorb ions such as magnesium.

Explain why magnesium ions cannot be absorbed by diffusion.

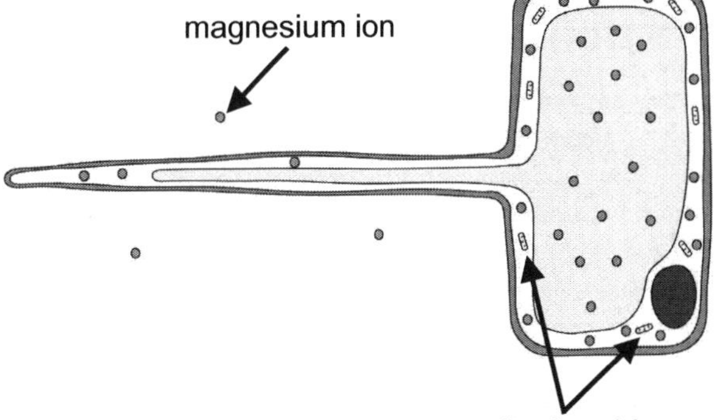


**b.** Why do plants need magnesium ions?

**c.** How are root hair cells adapted to carry out active transport?

# Chapter 2: Organisation

| |
|---|
| • State what is meant by a tissue, organ and organ system, giving examples. |
| • Describe the purpose of digestion and label the major parts of the digestive system. |
| • State the roles of the different parts of the digestive system. |
| • Describe the lock and key theory of enzyme action. |
| • Describe the structures of proteins, starch and lipids. |
| • Describe how to test for starch, reducing sugars, proteins and lipids (required practical). |
| • Describe and explain the effects of temperature and pH on enzymes. |
| • Describe how to investigate the effect of pH on the enzyme amylase (required practical). |
| • Describe how the small intestine is adapted for efficient absorption of molecules. |
| • Describe what is meant by a double circulatory system and the advantages of this. |
| • Describe the structure of the human heart including blood vessels and valves. |
| • Describe the movement of blood through the human heart. |
| • Describe the functions and structures of arteries, veins and capillaries. |
| • Describe the parts of the blood and the functions of these. |
| • Describe different cardiovascular diseases and how they are treated. |
| • Describe how the human lungs are adapted for efficient gas exchange. |
| • Describe how cancers form and the risk factors for cancer. |
| • Describe how different diseases can be triggered and how they can be linked. |
| • Describe how disease can be correlated to risk factors. |
| • Describe how lifestyle can lead to disease. |
| • Describe the roles of plant tissues including in the leaf, xylem, phloem and meristem. |
| • Describe what is meant by transpiration and the factors that can affect this. |

# The Digestive System

Exam tip: The digestive system can seen complicated. It is very important that you learn the names and functions of the different parts.

1. The diagram below shows a collection of muscle cells forming a muscle tissue.

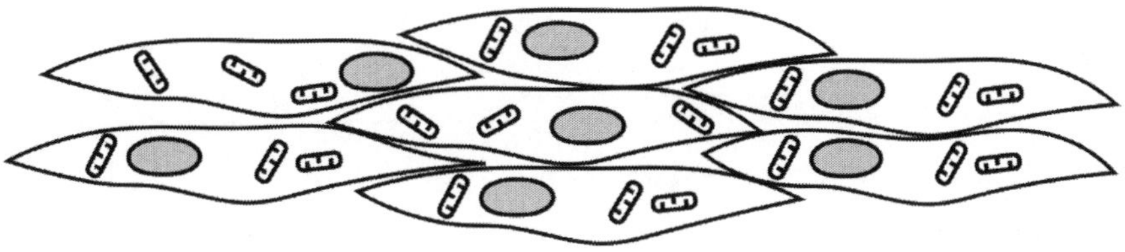

a. Which of the following is the function of muscle cells?

| | | |
|---|---|---|
| Muscle cells send electrical impulses around the body | Muscle cells fertilise an ovum during reproduction | Muscle cells contract (get shorter) |

b. Describe two ways that muscle cells are adapted to carry out their function.

c. In the diagram above, the muscle cells have formed a muscle tissue.

We find muscle tissue in organs and in organ systems.

Draw a line from the correct words on the left to the correct definition on the right.

| | |
|---|---|
| Tissue | This is a collection of organs working together to carry out a function. A good example is the digestive system. Organ systems form an organism. |
| Organ | This is a group of cells with a similar structure and function. |
| Organ system | This is a group of tissues working together for a specific function. The stomach is a good example. This contains muscle tissue and glandular tissue. |

**2.** Complete the following paragraph using the words below.

| | | | | | |
|---|---|---|---|---|---|
| **enzymes** | **proteins** | **smaller** | **bloodstream** | **large** | **absorbed** |

Food molecules such as carbohydrates, lipids and ____________________ are too ______________ to be absorbed directly into the ____________________. Because of this, they have to be digested. In digestion, ____________________ are used to break down large food molecules into ______________ soluble molecules. These smaller molecules can then be ____________________ into the bloodstream.

**3.** The human digestive system is shown in the diagram.

Label the diagram using the labels below.

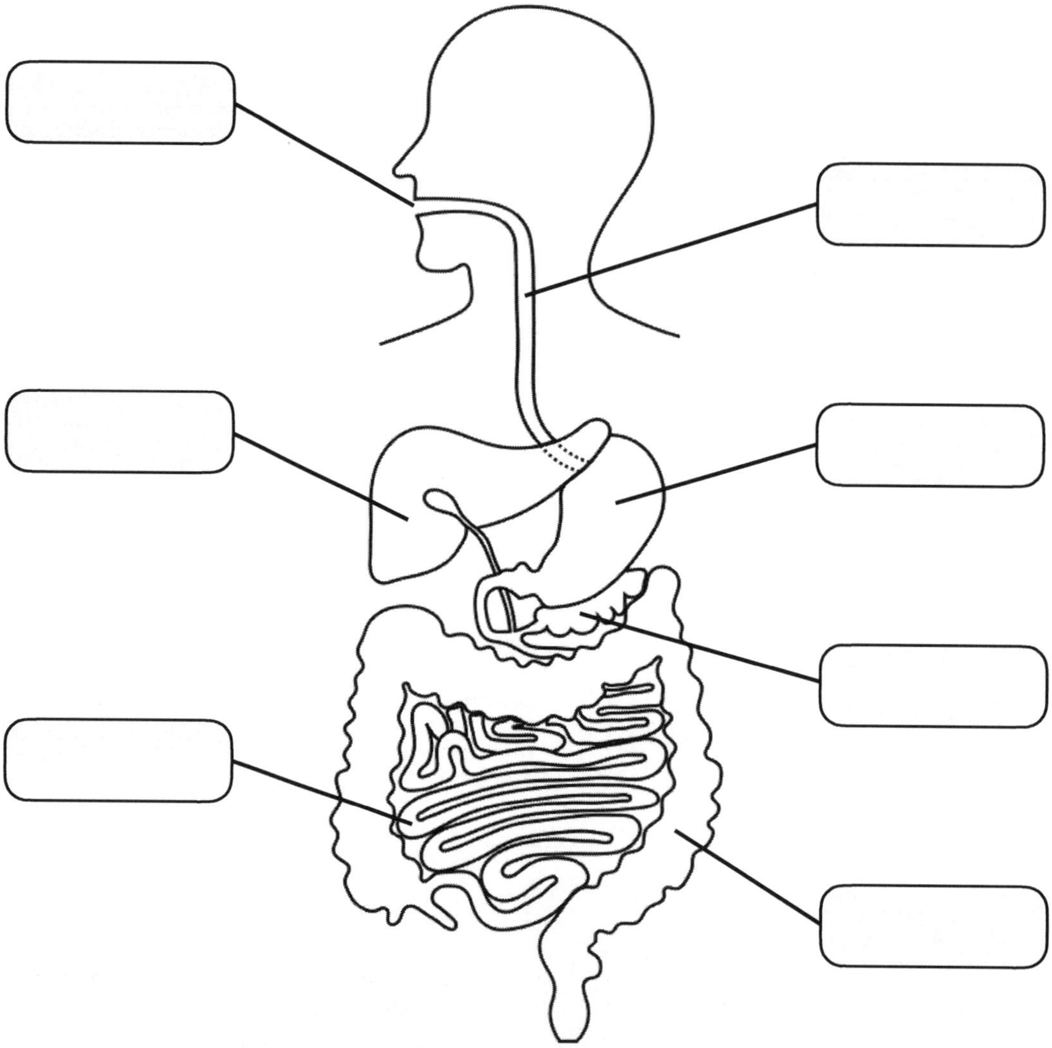

| | | | |
|---|---|---|---|
| oesophagus | small intestine | pancreas | stomach |
| liver | large intestine | mouth | |

**4.** The flow-chart shows how food passes through the digestive system.

Answer the questions about each part of the digestive system.

mouth → oesophagus → stomach → small intestine → large intestine

**mouth**

**a.** First food is chewed in the mouth and mixed with saliva.

Describe the role of the enzymes in the saliva.

**oesophagus**

**b.** Describe the function of the oesophagus.

**stomach**

**c.** Which type of food molecule starts its digestion in the stomach?

**d.** What is the function of the hydrochloric acid in the stomach?

**e.** Over several hours muscles in the stomach churn the food into a fluid.

Explain why this is important.

**small intestine**

**f.** The pancreas releases fluid into the small intestine.

Describe the functions of the enzymes in this fluid.

**g.** The liver releases bile into the small intestine.

Describe two roles of bile in the digestive system.

**h.** The walls of the small intestine release enzymes.

What is the function of these enzymes?

**i.** Describe how the products of digestion are absorbed into the bloodstream.

**large intestine**

**j.** What is the role of the large intestine?

**5.** Describe what happens to the products of digestion once they are absorbed into the bloodstream.

# Digestive Enzymes

**1.** Enzymes play a key role in the digestive system.

**a.** The diagram shows an enzyme breaking down a molecule into two product molecules.

Label the diagram using the labels below.

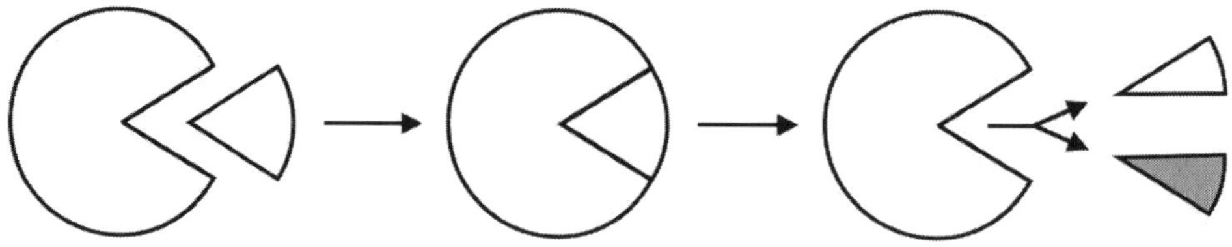

| enzyme | substrate | active site | substrate attached to active site | products |
|---|---|---|---|---|

**b.** The diagram shows the same enzyme and a different substrate molecule.

Explain why the enzyme cannot break down this molecule.

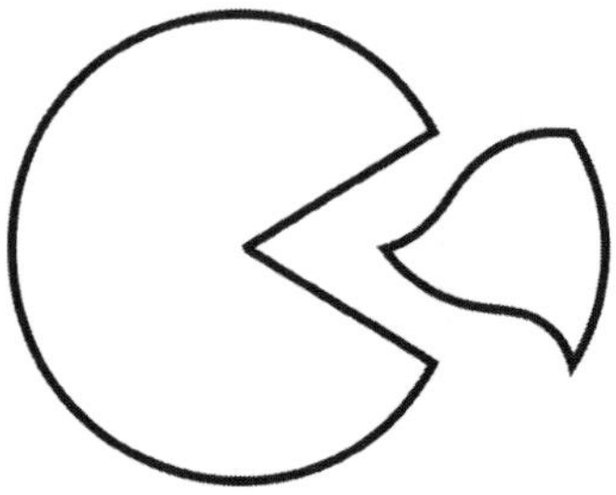

**c.** What is meant by the lock and key theory?

Exam tip: Another theory for enzyme action is the "induced fit" theory. In this theory, the active site is not a fixed shape but instead moulds itself around the substrate molecule.

**2.** The structure of a protein is shown in the diagram.

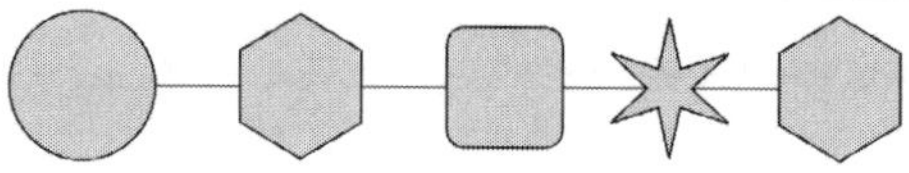

**a.** A protein is a chain of amino acids. Label the diagram to show the amino acids.

**b.** How many different amino acids will be released when the above protein is digested? Explain your answer.

**c.** Proteins are digested by the enzyme protease. Where is protease found in the digestive system?

Circle the correct boxes.

| | | |
|---|---|---|
| mouth | stomach | pancreatic fluid |
| small intestine | liver | large intestine |

**d.** Describe what happens to the amino acids once they have been absorbed into the bloodstream.

**3.** Starch is an example of a carbohydrate.

The digestion of a starch molecule is shown in the diagram.

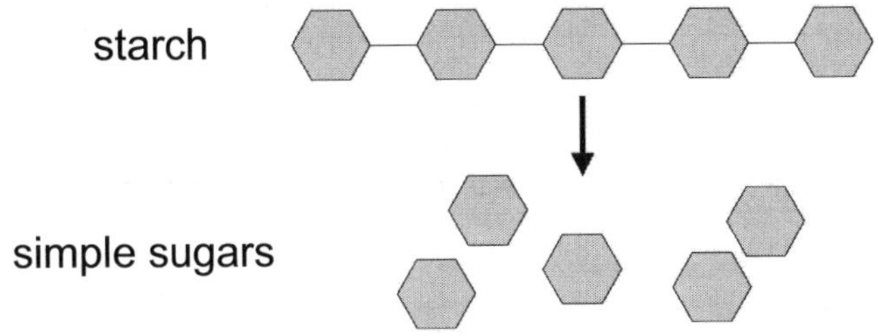


**a.** Describe the structure of a starch molecule.

**b.** Which type of enzyme is used in the human body to digest starch? Circle the correct box.

protease | lipase | carbohydrase

**c.** The specific enzyme that digests starch is called amylase.

Where is amylase found in the digestive system?

**4.** Lipids (fats) consist of three fatty acid molecules joined to a molecule of glycerol.

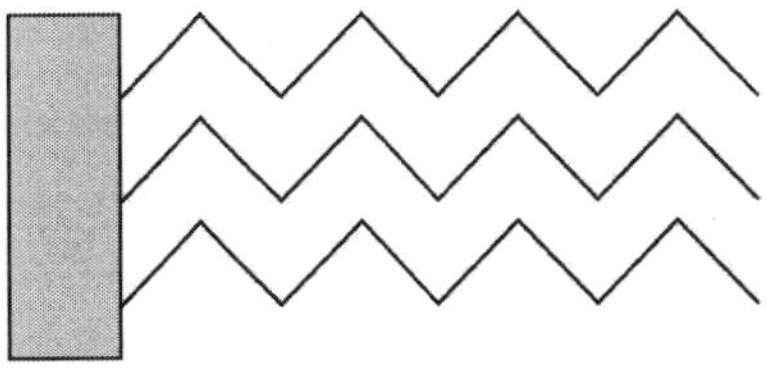

**a.** Label the lipid molecule shown on the right.

**b.** Lipids are digested by the enzyme lipase.

State the two locations of lipase in the digestive system.

**c.** The digestion of lipids is made faster by bile.

Complete the boxes to show where bile is produced and stored.

Bile is produced in the | Bile is stored in the

**d.** Bile emulsifies lipids. This is shown in the diagram on the right.

Describe what is meant by "emulsifies lipids" and explain how this increases the rate of lipid digestion.

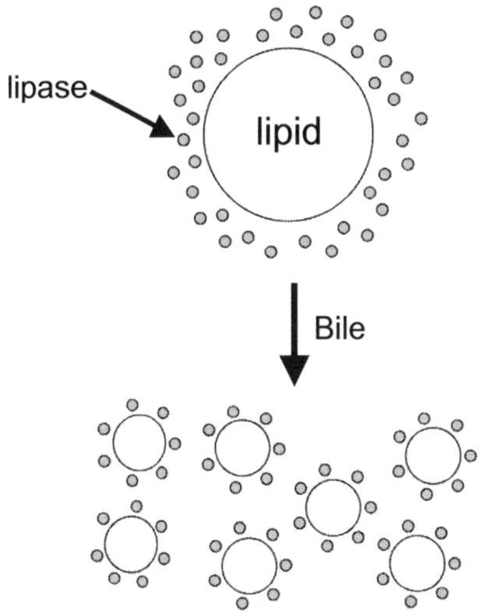


**e.** Bile is an alkaline fluid. Explain how this also increases the rate of lipid digestion.

# Required Practical: Food Tests

Exam tip: Please do not get hung up on learning the exact volumes of the solutions used in this practical. It is not necessary for the exam. You can also carry out the tests in any order.

**1.** Before we carry out food tests, we need to prepare our food sample.

**a.** Explain why safety goggles are essential during this practical.

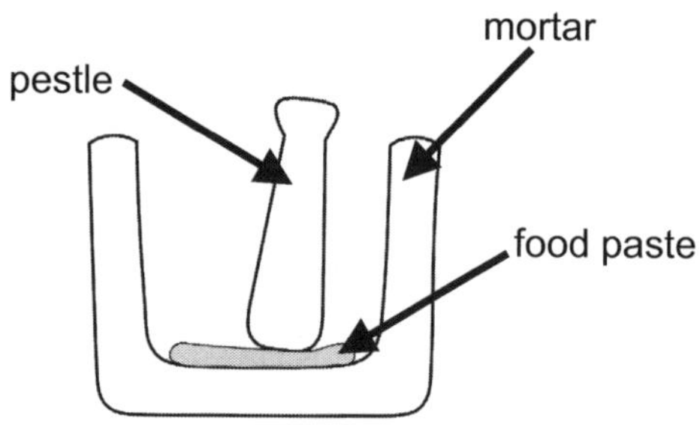


**b.** First we grind the food into a paste using a mortar and pestle and a small amount of distilled water.

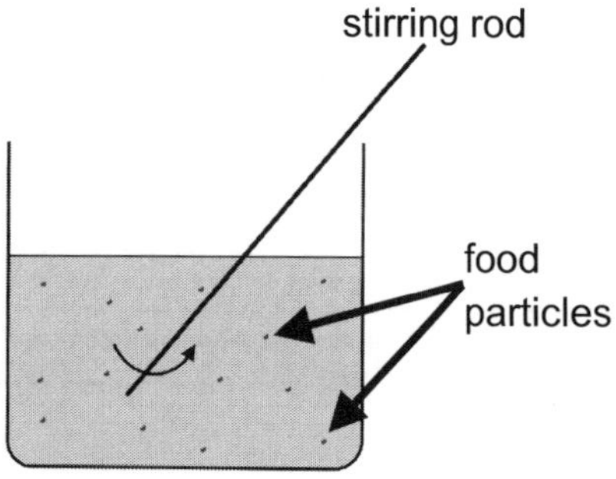


We then transfer the paste to a beaker. We then add more distilled water and stir.

Explain why we stir the sample.

**c.** Next we pass our solution through a filter.

Explain why this step is necessary.

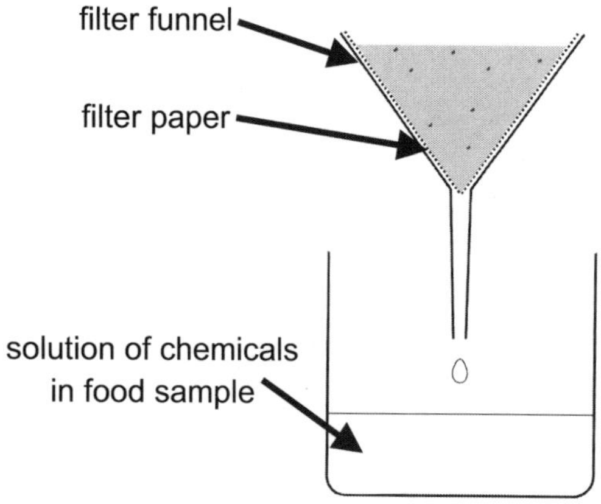


At this point, we can test our solution for the chemicals present in the food sample.

**2.** The first food test that we carry out is for starch, which is a carbohydrate.

**a.** First, we place a small volume of our food solution into a test tube.

We then add several drops of iodine solution. State the colour of iodine solution.

**b.** What colour change would we see if starch is present in the food sample?

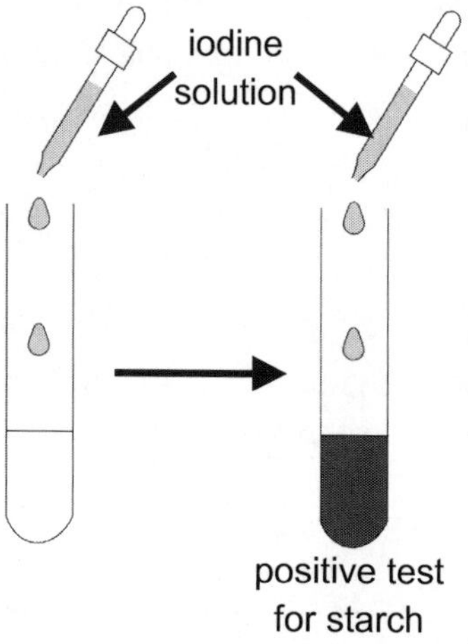

3. Reducing sugars (such as glucose) are another type of carbohydrate.

To test for reducing sugars we first add several drops of Benedict's solution to our food solution.

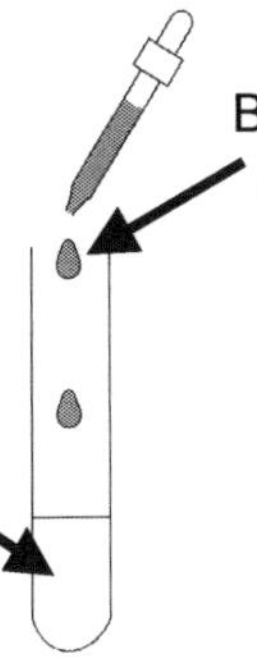


a. What colour is Benedict's solution? Circle the correct box.

blue | orange | green

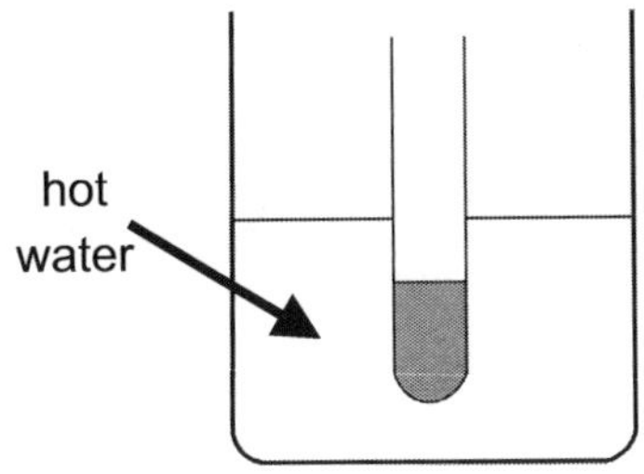


**b.** We now place the test tube into a beaker and half-fill the beaker with hot water from a kettle.

We leave the test tube in the hot water for five minutes. If reducing sugars are present then the Benedict's solution will change colour.

State how the colour of Benedict's solution changes depending on the amount of reducing sugar present.

| small amount of sugar present | more sugar present | a lot of sugar present |
| --- | --- | --- |
| colour change = | colour change = | colour change = |

**c.** Remember that the Benedict's test only works with reducing sugars such as glucose.

The Benedict's test does not work with non-reducing sugars.
State an example of a non-reducing sugar.

**4.** To test for proteins, we add several drops of Biuret solution to our food solution. This is shown in the diagram.

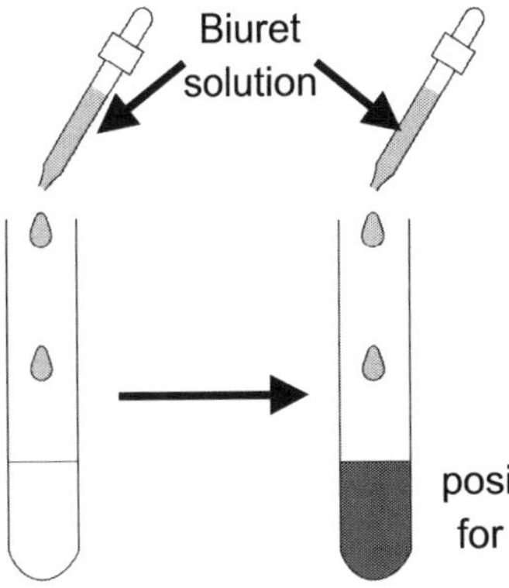


**a.** State the colour of Biuret solution before we add this to the food solution.

**b.** Which colour does Biuret change to if there is protein present?

**5.** The final food test is for lipids.

How do we prepare our food sample differently when testing for lipids?

To test for lipids, we add a small amount of ethanol and a small amount of distilled water to our food solution. We then shake the test tube. If lipids are present, a white cloudy suspension forms.

The original lipid test from AQA was based on Sudan III. This test has now been withdrawn due to safety issues. You need to learn the ethanol test for lipids as described above.

# Effect of Temperature and pH on Enzymes

**1.** Temperature has a dramatic effect on how rapidly an enzyme works.

**a.** The graph below shows the effect of changing the temperature on the rate of an enzyme-catalysed reaction.

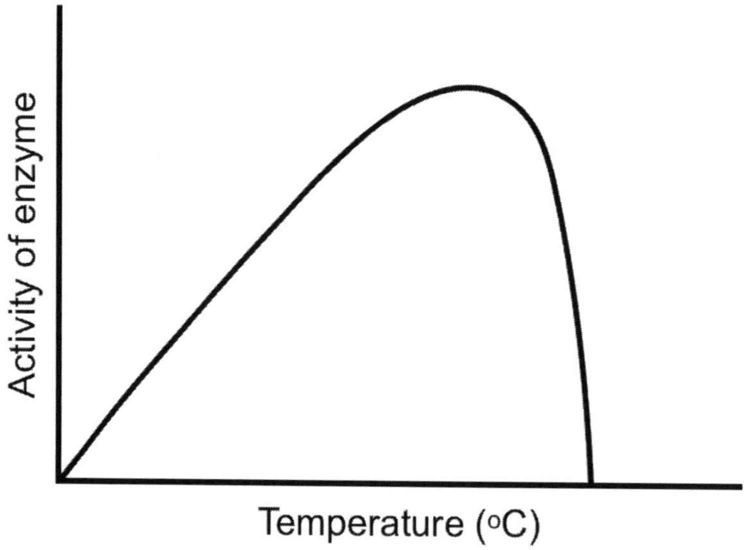


Complete the paragraph using the words below.

**maximum** **increases** **zero** **substrate** **faster** **collisions** **optimum** **denatured**

As we increase the temperature, the reaction gets faster as the activity of the enzyme ____________________. At higher temperatures, the enzyme and ____________________ are moving ____________________. This means that there are more ____________________ per second between the substrate and the active site. At the ____________________ temperature, the enzyme is working at its fastest rate and there are the ____________________ frequency of collisions between the substrate and the active site. Past the optimum temperature, the activity of the enzyme falls to __________ This is because at high temperatures the enzyme molecule vibrates and the active site changes shape. Scientists say that the enzyme is ____________________. Now the substrate no longer fits perfectly into the active site so the reaction stops.

**b.** Mark the following points on the graph:

- The optimum temperature
- Where the enzyme is denatured

2. The lock and key theory can be used to explain the effect of temperature on enzymes.

Complete the diagram to show the effect of high temperatures on an enzyme.

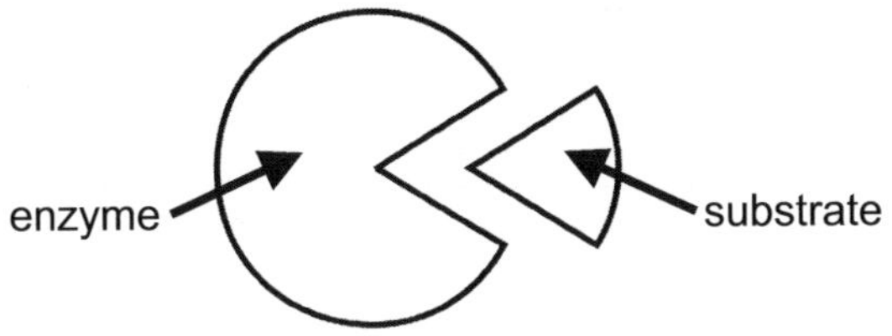


Optimum temperature: active site is perfectly shaped to fit the substrate

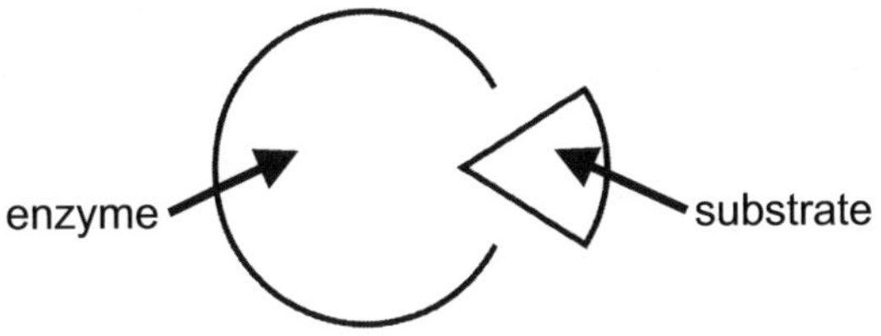


High temperature:

3. Enzymes are also affected by the pH.

a. The graph below shows the effect of changing the pH on the rate of an enzyme-catalysed reaction.

On the graph, label the optimum pH for this enzyme.

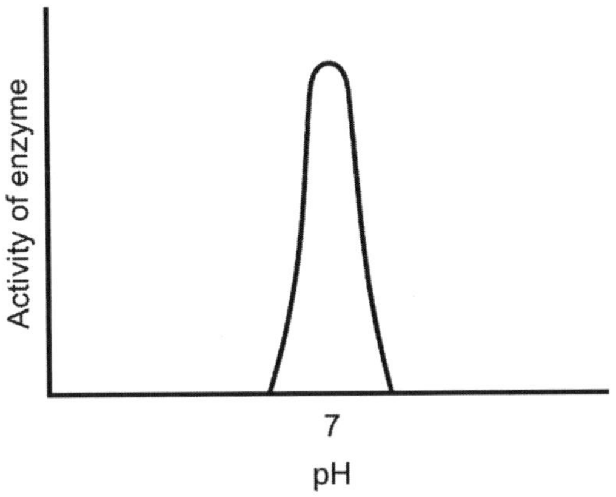


b. The enzyme protease is found in the stomach. Draw a line on the graph to show the effect of pH on protease.

c. The enzyme lipase is found in the small intestine. Draw a line on the graph to show the effect of pH on lipase.

d. Complete the sentences below by selecting the correct word.

Stomach enzymes such as protease work better in [acidic / neutral / alkaline] conditions. However, enzymes found in the small intestine such as lipase work best in [acidic / neutral / alkaline] conditions.

e. Explain why enzymes do not work well if the pH is more acidic or more alkaline than their optimum pH.

# Required Practical: Effect of pH on Amylase

**1.** The diagram on the right shows the action of amylase.

Describe the role of amylase in the digestive system.

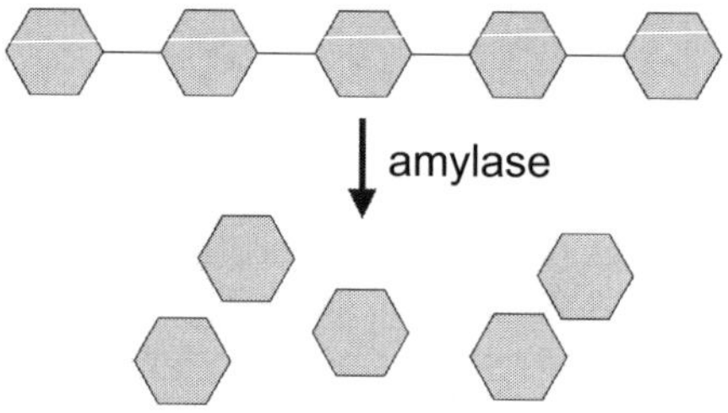


**2.** We are going to investigate the effect of pH on amylase.

First we place one drop of iodine into each well of a spotting tile.

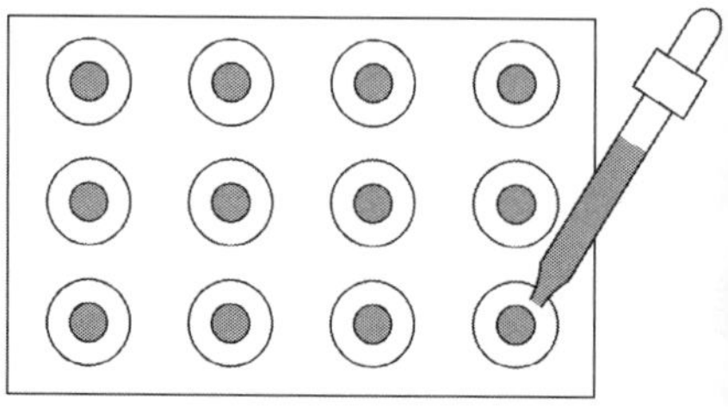

**a.** Complete the sentence below to show how iodine reacts with starch.

In the presence of starch, iodine goes from orange to [ ]

Exam tip: remember that you do not need to learn specific volumes

**b.** We now set up 3 test tubes as shown in the diagram.

One of the test tubes contains a buffer solution.

Explain what is meant by a buffer solution.

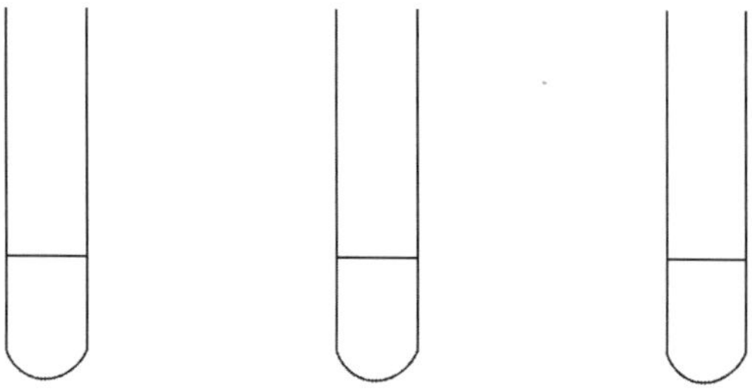

2 cm³ starch solution | 2 cm³ amylase solution | 2 cm³ pH 5 buffer solution

**c.** Next we place the three test tubes in a water bath at 30°C.

We leave the test tubes in the water for 10 minutes.

Why is it important that we leave the test tubes in the water bath for this time?

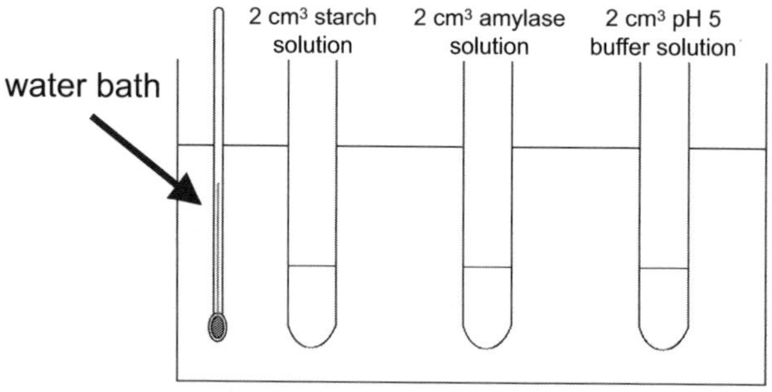


Now we combine the three solutions into one test tube and mix with a stirring rod.

We return the solution to the water bath and start a stopwatch.

At this point, the amylase will start to break down the starch.

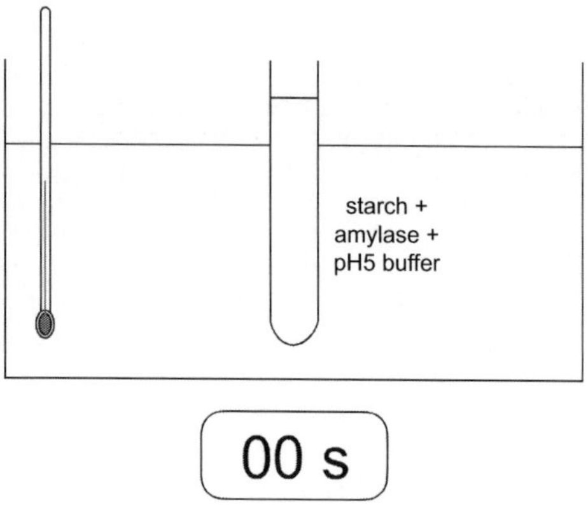

**d.** After thirty seconds, we use a stirring rod to transfer one drop of the solution to a well in the spotting tile which contains iodine solution.

What will happen to the colour of the iodine solution? Explain your answer.

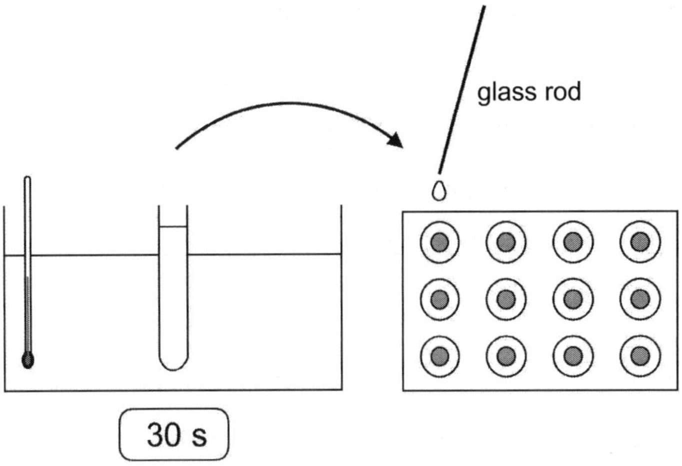


**e.** We continue taking samples every thirty seconds until there is no more starch present.

How can we tell when there is no more starch present?

We now repeat the whole experiment using different pH buffers to test a range of pHs.

Exam tip: In your exam, you could be asked to describe the problems with a practical. This practical has two main problems. It's worth learning these and the solutions to these problems.

**3. a.** We are only taking samples every thirty seconds.

Explain why this is a problem and how we could address this.

**b.** It can be difficult to tell when the reaction has finished.

Explain why this is difficult and how we can address this problem.

**4.** In every experiment, we have an independent variable, a dependent variable and control variables.

**a.** Complete the boxes to show the independent and dependent variables.

| Independent variable | Dependent variable |
| --- | --- |
| | |

**b.** State the control variables in this experiment.

# Absorption in the Small Intestine

**1.** In digestion, enzymes break down large food molecules into smaller soluble molecules.

These smaller soluble molecules are then absorbed into the bloodstream in the small intestine.

**a.** Circle the correct box to show the length of the small intestine in humans.

| 3 m | 4 m | 5 m |
|---|---|---|

**b.** Why is it important that the small intestine is so long?

**2.** The diagram below shows the lining of the small intestine.

**a.** Label the diagram to show the villi, microvilli and blood vessels.

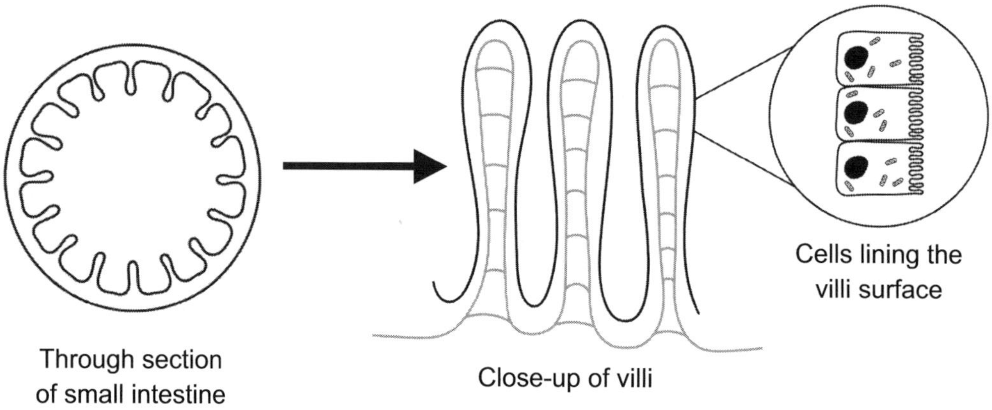


**b.** Explain how the following features increase the rate of diffusion of small soluble molecules into the bloodstream.

| Villi and microvilli | Good blood supply | Thin membrane on the villi |
|---|---|---|
| | | |

**c.** Molecules which cannot be absorbed by diffusion are absorbed by active transport. These include simple sugars.

The diagram shows a close-up of the cells lining the surface of the villi.

Explain why these cells have a large number of mitochondria.

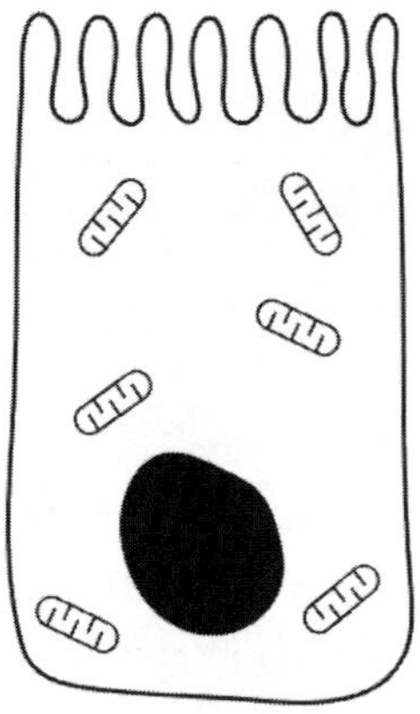

# The Heart and Circulation

Exam tip: It's definitely worth learning the definitions of the single and double circulatory systems as well as the blood vessels of the human heart.

**1.** Fish have a single circulatory system. This is shown in the diagram below.

**a.** Draw arrows to show the pathway of blood flow in the single circulatory system.

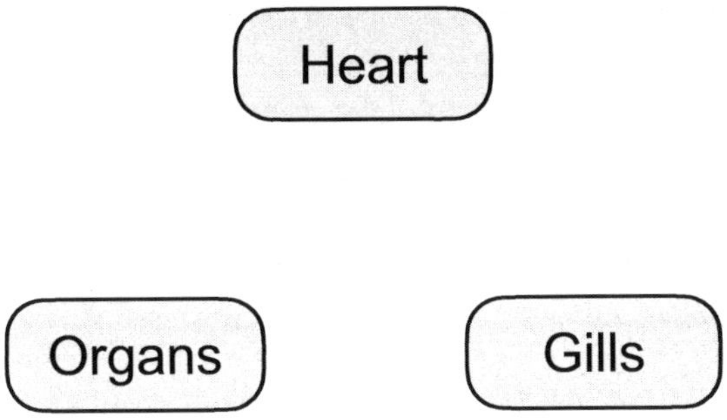


**b.** Label the arrows to show the oxygenated blood and the deoxygenated blood.

**c.** Explain why this is called a single circulatory system.

**d.** Describe what happens to the blood when it passes through the gills.

**e.** How does the blood change when it passes through the organs?

**f.** Describe the disadvantage of the single circulatory system.

**2.** Humans have a double circulatory system. This is shown in the diagram below.

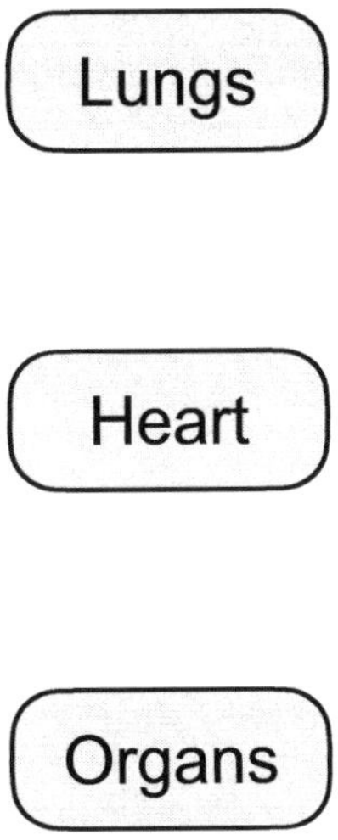


**a.** Draw arrows to show the pathway of blood flow.

**b.** Label the arrows to show the oxygenated blood and the deoxygenated blood.

**c.** Explain why this is called a double circulatory system.

**d.** Describe the advantage of the double circulatory system.

**3.** The diagram shows the structure of the human heart.

**a.** Which type of tissue is the heart formed from?

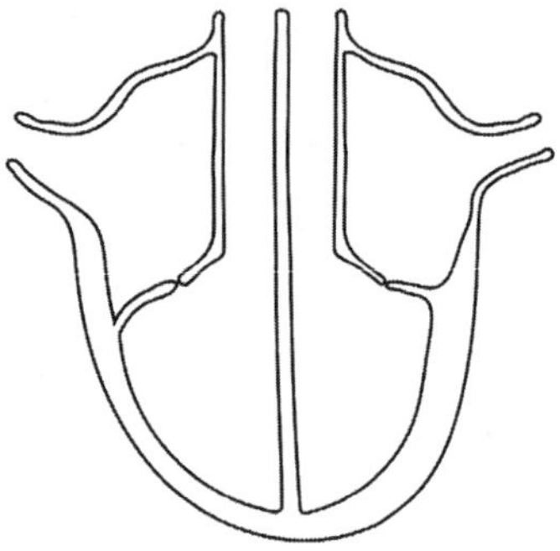

**b.** Label the diagram of the heart using the labels below.

Left atrium | Left ventricle | Right atrium | Right ventricle | Valves

**c.** Complete the diagram to show the function of each blood vessel.

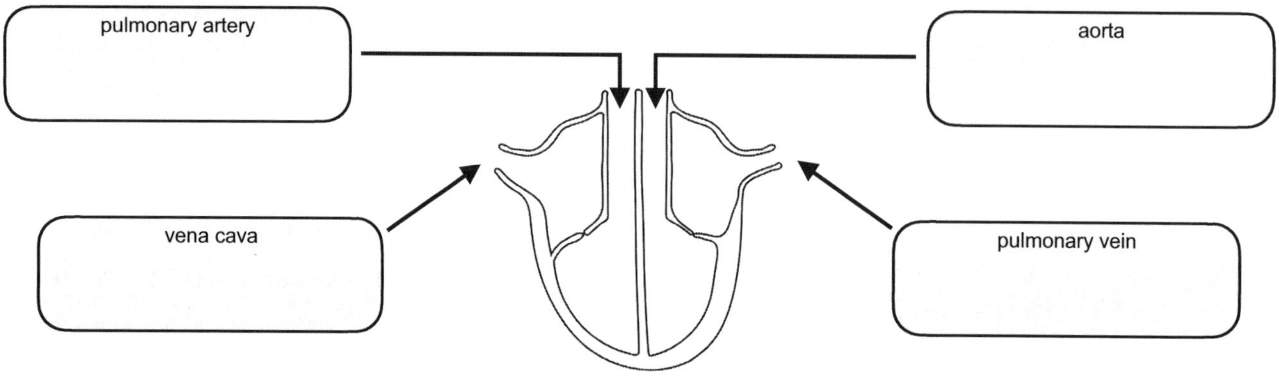


**d.** The diagrams below show the pathway of blood through the heart.

Complete the boxes to show what is happening at each stage.

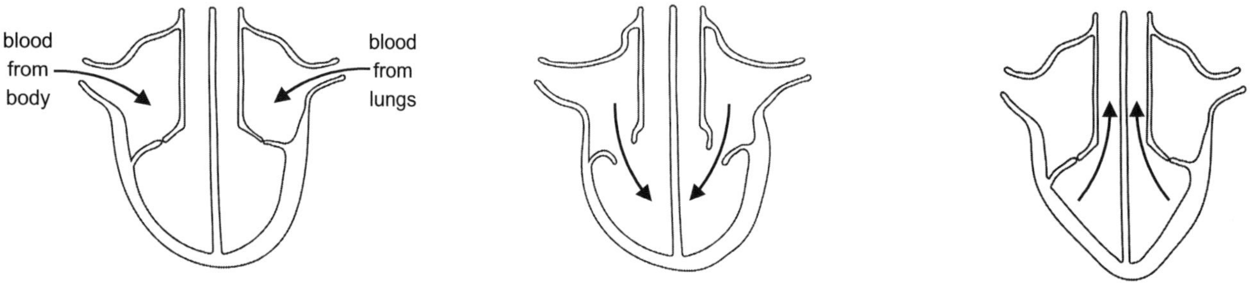


**e.** Describe the role of the valves between the atria and the ventricles.

**f.** What is the role of the coronary artery?

**4.** Describe the role of the pacemaker in the heart and of artificial pacemakers.

| Role of pacemaker | Role of artificial pacemaker |
| --- | --- |
| | |

# Arteries, Veins and Capillaries

**1.** The human circulatory system is shown below.

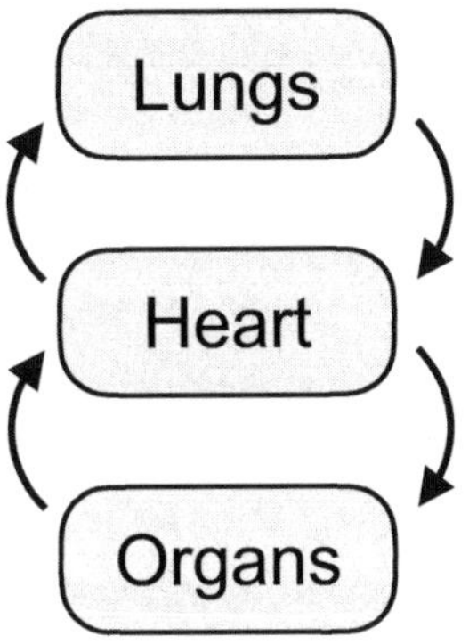


**a.** Label the diagram to show the arteries and the veins.

**b.** Complete the boxes below to show which blood vessels carry oxygenated blood and which carry deoxygenated blood?

| Arteries | Veins |
|---|---|
| oxygenated / deoxygenated blood | oxygenated / deoxygenated blood |

**c.** Where do we find capillaries?

**2.** The diagram shows the structure of arteries.

**a.** Which of the following are true about blood flow through arteries?

- Blood flows from the heart to the organs
- Blood flows from the organs to the heart
- Blood is at a high pressure
- Blood is at a low pressure
- Blood travels in surges (pulses)

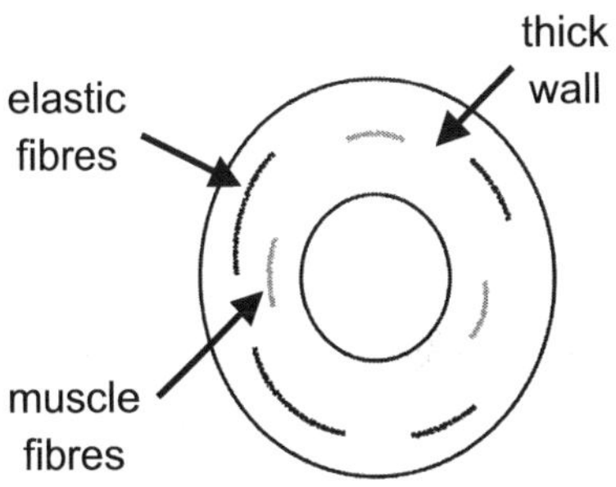


**b.** Explain why arteries have thick muscular walls and elastic fibres.

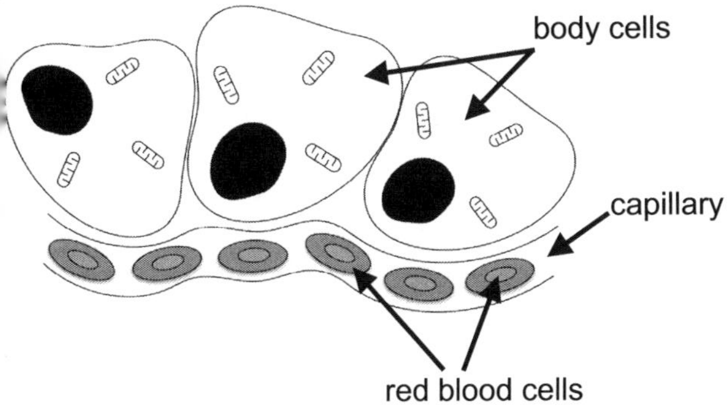


**3.** The diagram on the left shows the structure of capillaries.

**a.** Describe the function of capillaries.

**b.** How are the capillaries adapted to carry out this function?

**4.** Veins carry deoxygenated blood from the organs back to the heart.

The diagram on the right shows the structure of veins.

**a.** Explain why veins have a thin wall.

**b.** Describe the purpose of the valves in veins.

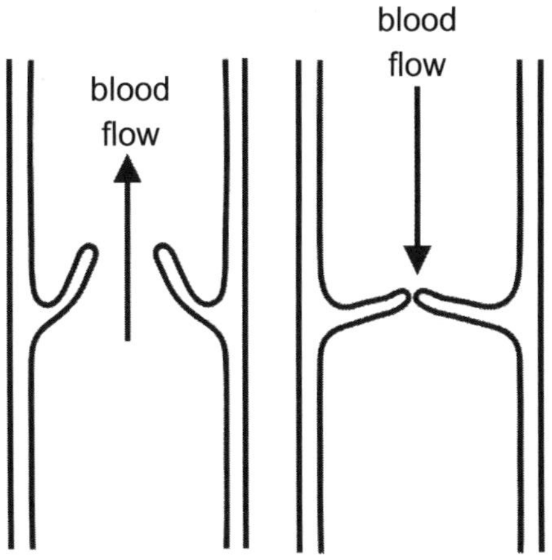

# The Blood

**1.** Human blood contains four major parts. One of these is blood plasma.

Complete the following paragraph using the words below.

**digestion  lungs  urine  liquid  starch  urea  dissolved  aerobic  kidneys  small**

The blood plasma is the ________________ part of the blood. The purpose of blood plasma is to transport ________________ substances around the body. Molecules produced during ________________ are transported from the ________________ intestine to body cells. This includes glucose which is produced when ________________ is digested. Carbon dioxide is also transported in blood plasma. Carbon dioxide is produced by cells when they carry out ________________ respiration. The carbon dioxide is carried to the ________________ where it is breathed out. Finally, blood plasma carries the waste product ________________ . This is produced by the liver and transported in the plasma to the ________________ to be excreted in ________________ .

**2.** The blood contains a large number of red blood cells.

**a.** Red blood cells transport oxygen from the lungs to body cells. To do this, they contain the molecule haemoglobin. Complete the equations below to show how haemoglobin works.

oxygen + haemoglobin —lungs→ [          ]

oxyhaemoglobin —organs→ [          ] + [          ]

**b.** Red blood cells are adapted to carry oxygen around the body.

These adaptations are shown in the diagram.

Complete the boxes to describe the purposes of the adaptations shown.

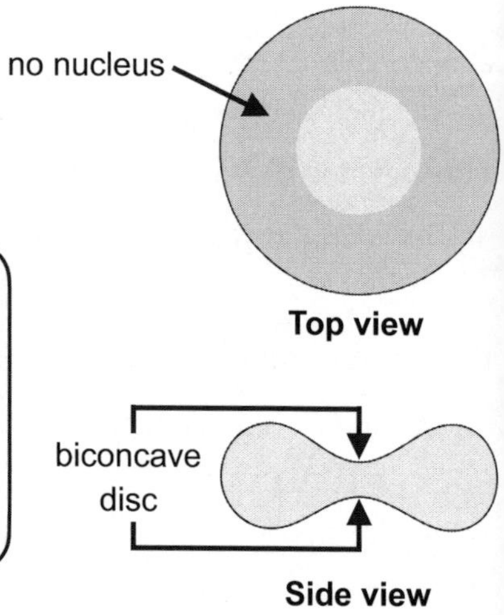


| No nucleus | Biconcave disc |
| --- | --- |
| | |

3. Human blood also contains a small number of white blood cells.

You will see more about white blood cells in the chapter on Infection and Response.

The diagram shows two typical white blood cells.

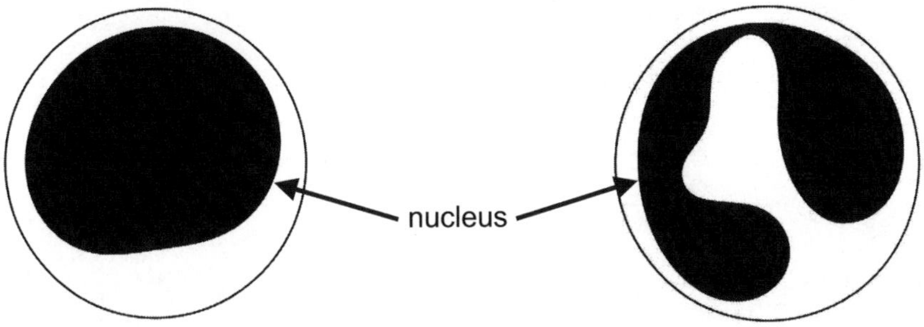


a. Describe the role of white blood cells in the human body.

b. Unlike red blood cells, white blood cells contain a nucleus.

Describe the role of the nucleus in white blood cells.

4. The final part of human blood are platelets. These are tiny fragments of cells.

a. Which of the following are the function of platelets?

- Transport oxygen from the lungs to the cells
- Help to fight infectious diseases
- Help the blood to clot

b. In certain types of leukaemia, the number of platelets can fall.

One of the symptoms of this is an increased risk of bleeding. Suggest why this is the case.

5. Blood and blood products are used a lot in medicine.

a. Describe three uses of blood and blood products in medicine.

- 
- 
- 

b. What are the risks when using blood or blood products?

# Cardiovascular Diseases

**1.** Cardiovascular diseases are diseases of the heart and blood vessels.

**a.** Cardiovascular diseases are non-communicable. What is meant by this?

**b.** Coronary heart disease is an example of a cardiovascular disease.

Which of the following statements is true about the coronary arteries?

The coronary arteries branch out of the pulmonary artery and provide oxygen to the muscle cells of the heart

The coronary arteries branch out of the aorta and provide carbon dioxide to the muscle cells of the heart

The coronary arteries branch out of the aorta and provide oxygen to the muscle cells of the heart

**c.** Explain why the heart muscle cells cannot contract effectively if the coronary arteries are blocked.

**d.** The diagram shows a coronary artery in a patient with coronary heart disease.

Remember that the lumen is the space where the blood flows.

Describe what happens in coronary heart disease and explain the effect of this on the heart muscle.

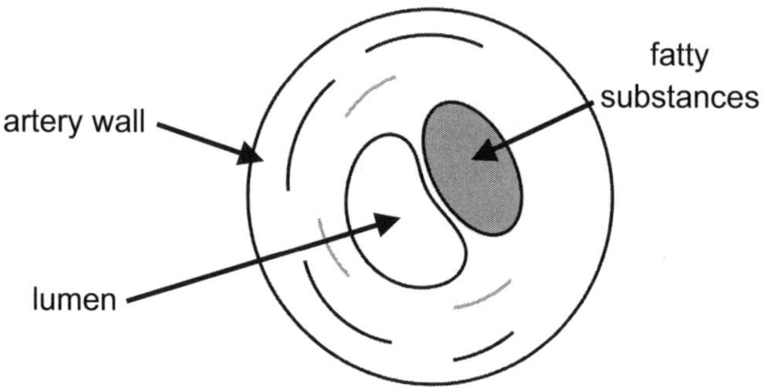


**e.** Many patients with coronary heart disease take drugs called statins.

Complete the boxes below to show the positive and negative effects of taking statins.

| Positive effects of taking statins | Negative effects of taking statins |
| --- | --- |
| | |

**f.** Patients with advanced coronary heart disease can be fitted with a stent. This is shown in the diagram.

Describe how a stent works.

**g.** Describe the disadvantage of stents.

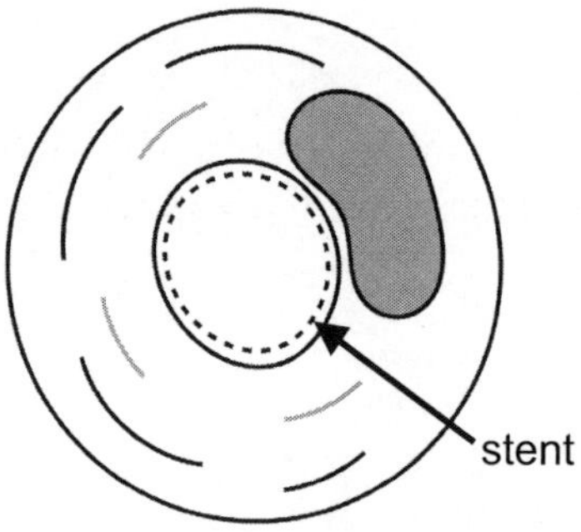

2. Some patients have problems with their heart valves. These are shown in the diagram below.

a. Beneath each diagram, describe the effect of the problem on the patient.

Heart valves do not open fully when the atria contract

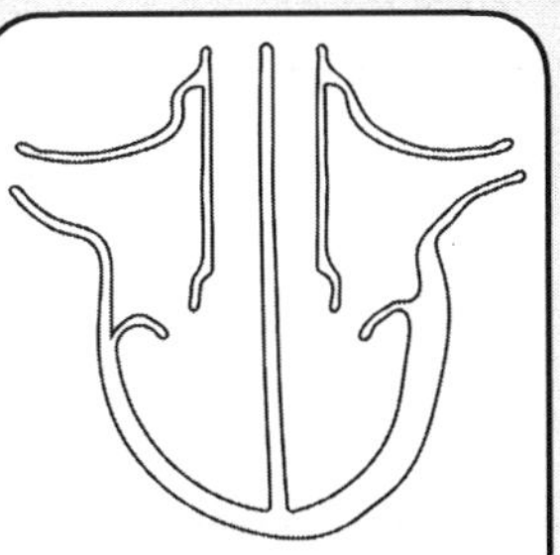

normal heart

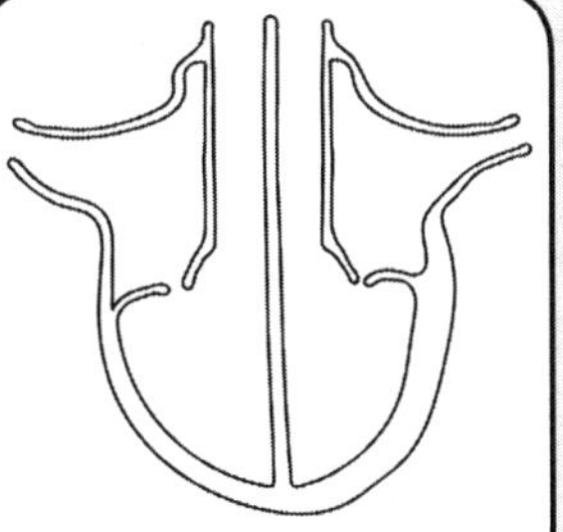

defective valves

Effect on patient:

Heart valves that leak blood when the ventricles contract

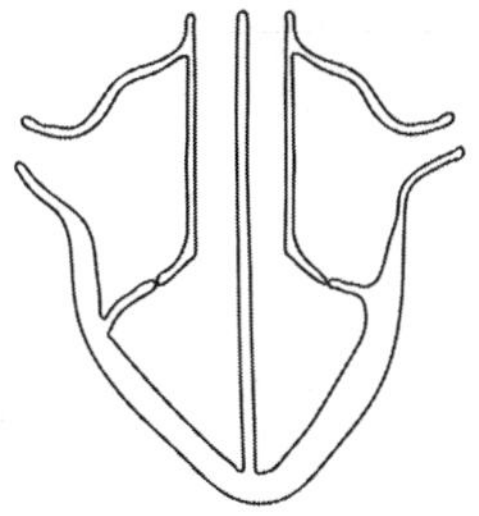

normal heart

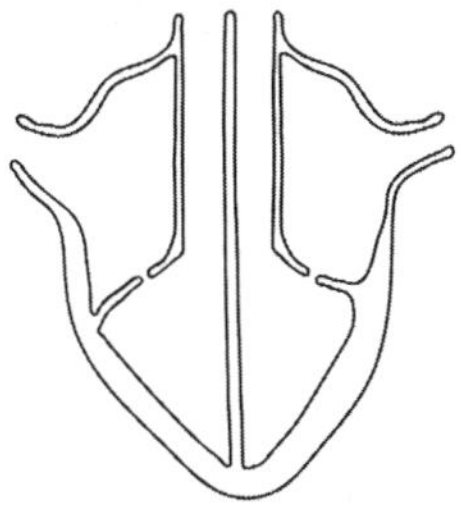

leaky valves

Effect on patient:

**b.** Defective heart valves can be treated using either mechanical valves or valves from animals.

Draw two lines from each type of valve to the correct description.

| Mechanical valves | Valves from animals |
|---|---|

| Do not last as long and may need to be replaced | Risk of blood clotting. Patient needs to take anti-clotting drugs for rest of life | These can last a lifetime | Patients are not required to take drugs with this type of valve |
|---|---|---|---|

**3.** In some cases, patients experience heart failure.

**a.** What is the problem with the heart in heart failure?

**b.** Patients with heart failure can be treated with a heart transplant or a heart-lung transplant.

Describe two problems with this.

**c.** Some patients with heart failure can be treated with an artificial heart.

Explain why artificial hearts can only be used for a relatively short time.

# Gas Exchange in the Lungs

**1.** The lungs are where gases such as oxygen and carbon dioxide are exchanged between the air and the blood.

A diagram of the lungs is shown below.

Label the diagram showing the key structures and their functions.

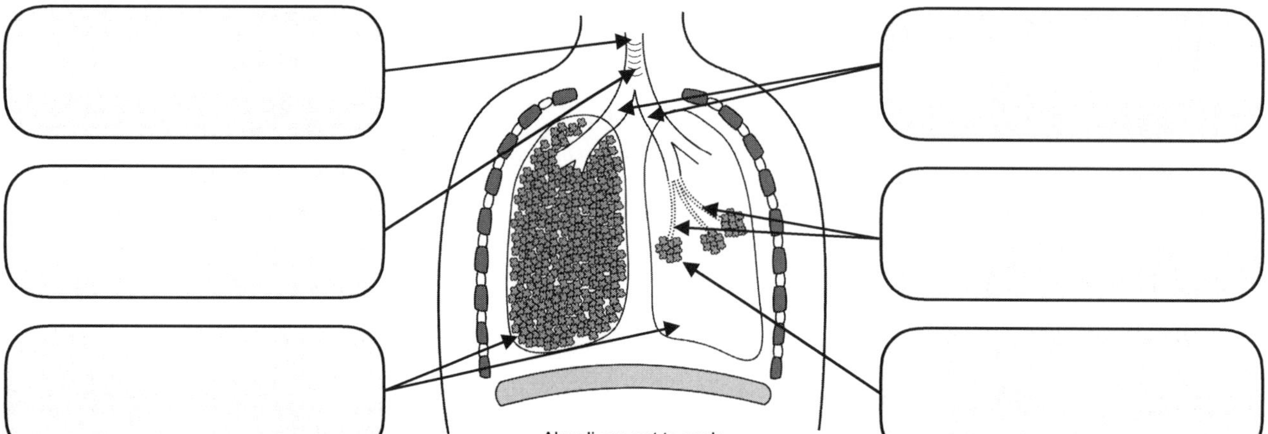

Alveoli are not to scale

**2.** The alveoli are critical for gas exchange.

The diagram below shows a single alveolus and a capillary.

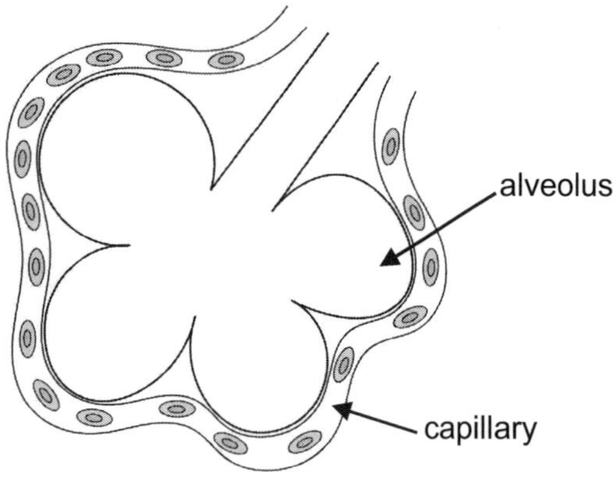


**a.** Label the diagram to show how gases move in and out of the blood.

**b.** Which process is used by the gases to move?

Select one answer only.

osmosis | diffusion | active transport

**c.** There are several ways that the lungs are adapted to ensure a rapid diffusion of gases in and out of the blood.

For each adaptation below, explain how this increases the rate of gas diffusion.

Each lung contains millions of alveoli

Alveoli have very thin walls

Alveoli have a very efficient blood supply

Breathing brings in oxygen and takes away carbon dioxide

# Cancer

**1.** As we saw in the Cell Biology chapter, cell division can take place by mitosis.

**a.** Complete the sentences by selecting the correct words from the boxes.

In cell division by mitosis, one cell is copied into [two / three / four] identical cells. Mitosis takes place during [growth / reproduction / death] and during repair eg after an injury. Mitosis is very tightly controlled by genes which are found in the [cytoplasm. / nucleus. / mitochondria.] These genes tell the cell when to divide and when to stop dividing.

**b.** The genes that control mitosis sometimes change. Now mitosis is uncontrolled and can lead to a tumour. Describe what is meant by a tumour.

The diagrams show a benign and a malignant tumour.

**Benign tumour**

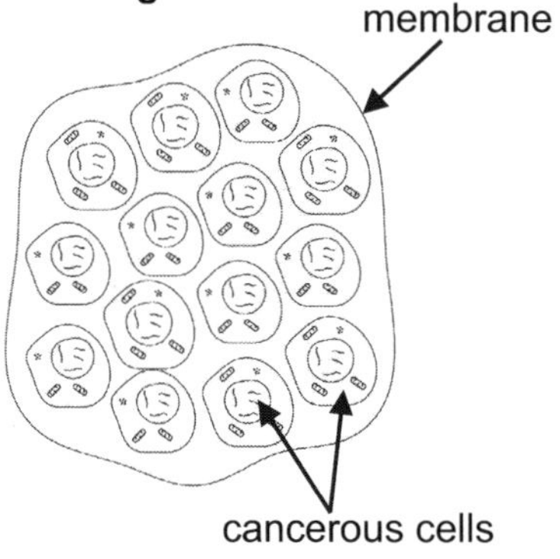


**c.** Benign tumours are generally less harmful to health than malignant tumours. Explain why this is the case.

**d.** Use the diagram to suggest why benign tumours remain in one location.

**e.** How do malignant tumours invade other locations?

**Malignant tumour**

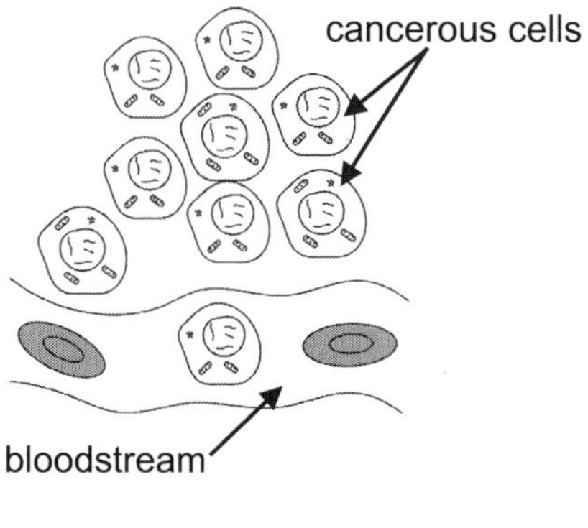


**f.** What is meant by a secondary tumour?

**g.** Suggest why malignant tumours are regarded as cancer but benign tumours are not.

Exam tip: Remember that the factors below do not cause cancer. They increase our risk of developing cancer over the course of our life.

**2.** There are a number of risk factors for cancer.

**a.** Some cancers are linked to genetics. What does this mean?

**b.** Other cancers are linked to our lifestyle.

State three lifestyle factors that can increase our risk of cancer.

**c.** Certain cancers are linked to substances in our environment.

One of these substances is radon.

Which of the following is true about radon?

| | | |
|---|---|---|
| Radon is found in the food that we eat | Radon is found in hygiene products eg deodorant | Radon is a radioactive gas that we breathe in |

**d.** Explain how radon increases the risk of developing cancer.

**e.** Suggest why radon increases the risk of lung cancer and not other types of cancer.

**f.** Draw lines to connect the risk factor and the correct type of cancer.

| | | |
|---|---|---|
| Breast cancer | Lung cancer | Cancer of the large intestine |

| | |
|---|---|
| Cancers linked to genetics | Cancers linked to lifestyle |

| | | |
|---|---|---|
| Cancer of the mouth and throat | Skin cancer | Prostate cancer |

# Communicable and Non-communicable Diseases

Exam tip: This topic is covered in both the Organisation part of the specification and also Infection and Response. It's really important to learn it.

**1.** Diseases can be caused by a range of different factors.

Complete the following paragraph using the words below.

**mental** **passed** **pathogens** **viruses** **measles** **heart disease** **stress** **pollution**

Good health involves a state of both physical and ________________ well being. Poor health can be caused by both communicable and non-communicable diseases. Communicable diseases can be ________________ from person to person via ________________ such as bacteria or ________________ . A good example of a communicable disease is ________________ .

Non-communicable diseases cannot be spread from person to person. A good example of a non-communicable disease is coronary ______________ . Poor health can also be caused by ______________, a poor diet or other factors eg ______________ .

**2.** Tick the correct boxes to show whether the diseases below are communicable or non-communicable.

| Disease | Communicable | Non-communicable |
|---|---|---|
| Measles | | |
| Cervical cancer | | |
| Human immunodeficiency virus (HIV) | | |
| Tuberculosis (TB) | | |
| Asthma | | |
| Depression | | |
| Human papilloma virus (HPV) | | |
| Dermatitis | | |
| Arthritis | | |
| Coronary heart disease | | |

**3.** Tuberculosis (TB) is a communicable lung disease caused by a bacterium.

**a.** Explain why most people who are exposed to the TB bacterium do not catch the disease.

**b.** Why are people with HIV more likely to catch TB than a person without HIV?

**4.** Sometimes one disease can be the cause of another disease.

Complete the sentences below by selecting the correct words from the boxes.

HPV is a relatively harmless communicable disease caused by a [fungus / virus / bacterium]. In women, infection with HPV can increase the risk of developing cancer of the [breast / ovaries / cervix].

**5.** Some diseases can be triggered by the immune system for example allergies.

**a.** Which of the following diseases are examples of allergies?

depression | asthma | dermatitis | measles

**b.** Describe how allergies can be triggered by the immune system.

**6.** Depression is an example of a mental illness.

**a.** Describe what is meant by a mental illness.

**b.** Arthritis is a physical illness as it affects the body.

People who develop arthritis can go on to develop depression.

Describe how arthritis can lead to depression.

# Correlating Risk Factors

**1.** Many diseases are non-communicable. A good example is lung cancer.

In the 1930s, lung cancer cases began to increase. Scientists tried to find the cause.

**a.** Why could scientists not carry out experiments on humans?

**b.** Instead, scientists carried out epidemiology.

Explain what is meant by epidemiology.

Scientists investigated how a person's risk of developing lung cancer depends on the number of cigarettes smoked per day and the number of years a person smoked. The results are shown in the scattergraphs below.

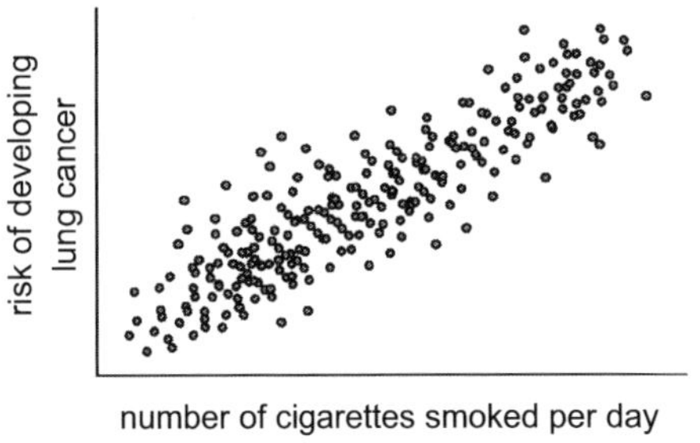


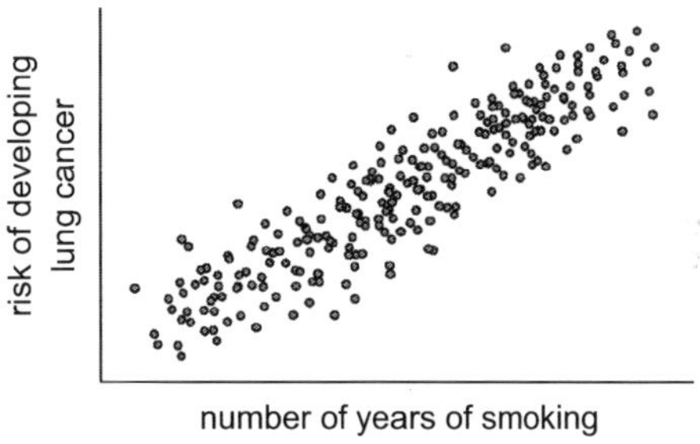


**c.** These scattergraphs show a positive correlation between the risk of developing lung cancer and the number of cigarettes smoked per day / number of years smoking.

What is meant by a positive correlation?

**d.** Explain how these scattergraphs do not show that lung cancer is caused by smoking.

**e.** Scientists now looked at how smoking could cause lung cancer. This is called a causal mechanism.

Describe the causal mechanism between smoking and lung cancer.

**f.** Epidemiology is based on sampling.

Explain the problem with biased sampling and how scientists attempt to overcome this.

# Lifestyle and Disease

**1.** Cardiovascular diseases are non-communicable disorders.

**a.** Explain how the following lifestyle factors increase your risk of cardiovascular diseases.

| A diet high in fat and low in vegetables | A diet high in salt |
|---|---|
| | |

**b.** Circle the correct words to describe how smoking and exercise effect your risk of cardiovascular diseases.

| Smoking | Regular Exercise |
|---|---|
| Increased / decreased risk of cardiovascular diseases | Increased / decreased risk of cardiovascular diseases |

**2.** Smoking causes a number of different non-communicable diseases.

**a.** Smoking can lead to lung cancer. This is because cigarette smoke contains carcinogens.

Explain what is meant by a carcinogen.

**b.** State another non-communicable disease caused by smoking.

**c.** Describe three possible effects that smoking while pregnant can have on an unborn child.

**3.** Drinking alcohol can have a number of negative effects on health.

**a.** Describe the effect of drinking alcohol while pregnant.

**b.** Describe three effects of excessive alcohol consumption on adults.

**4.** Type 2 diabetes is also caused by lifestyle factors.

**a.** Which of the following is a feature of type 2 diabetes (select one only)?

| | | | |
|---|---|---|---|
| Difficulty controlling blood pressure | Difficulty controlling heart rate | Difficulty controlling blood glucose levels | Difficulty controlling body temperature |

**b.** Describe how excessive alcohol consumption can indirectly lead to type 2 diabetes.

# Plant Tissues

**1.** Plants contain a number of organs. One of these is the leaf.

The diagram below shows a cross-section through a leaf.

Label the diagram using the labels below.

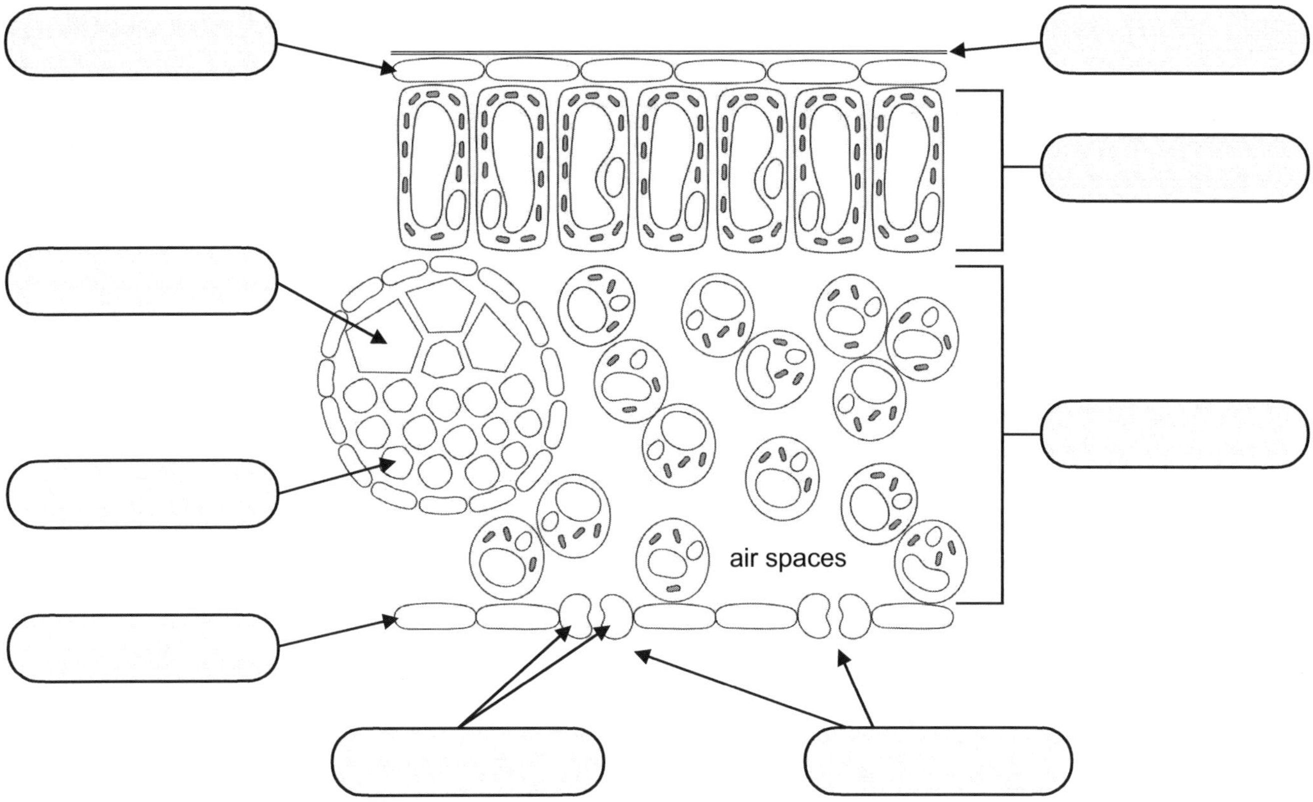


xylem | stomata | waxy cuticle | guard cells | phloem

lower epidermis | upper epidermis | palisade mesophyll | spongy mesophyll

**2.** The upper and lower surfaces of the leaf are covered with epidermal cells. These form epidermal tissue.

**a.** What is the role of the epidermal tissue?

**b.** Why is it important that the upper epidermis is transparent?

**c.** How is the upper epidermis adapted to reduce water loss from the leaf?

**d.** What is the role of the stomata on the lower epidermis?

**3.** In between the upper and lower epidermis, we find the mesophyll tissue.

**a.** The palisade mesophyll is found at the top of the leaf. What is the function of the palisade mesophyll?

**b.** The diagram shows the structure of a palisade mesophyll cell.

How are the palisade mesophyll cells adapted to carry out their role?

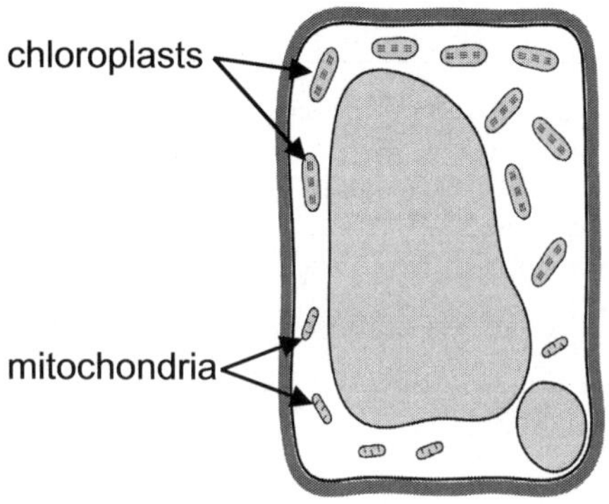


**c.** Suggest why the palisade mesophyll is located at the top of the leaf.

**d.** How is the spongy mesophyll adapted to carry out its function?

**e.** Draw arrows on the diagram on page 67 to show the diffusion of carbon dioxide and oxygen.

**4.** Xylem and phloem are two other important tissues found in plants.

**a.** Xylem tissue transports water from the roots to the stem and leaves.

How is the water used in the leaves?

**b.** Xylem tissue also transports dissolved minerals.

Give an example of a dissolved mineral transported in the xylem and states its function.

**c.** Phloem tissue carries out translocation. What is meant by this?

**d.** Describe two ways that the sugars carried in the phloem can be used by the plant.

**5.** Plants also contain meristem tissue.

**a.** Where in the plant do we find meristem tissue?

**b.** Meristem tissue contains plant stem cells. What is special about stem cells?

# Transpiration

**1.** Transpiration is an important process in plants.

Explain what is meant by transpiration.

**2.** The diagram on the right shows a cross-section through a leaf.

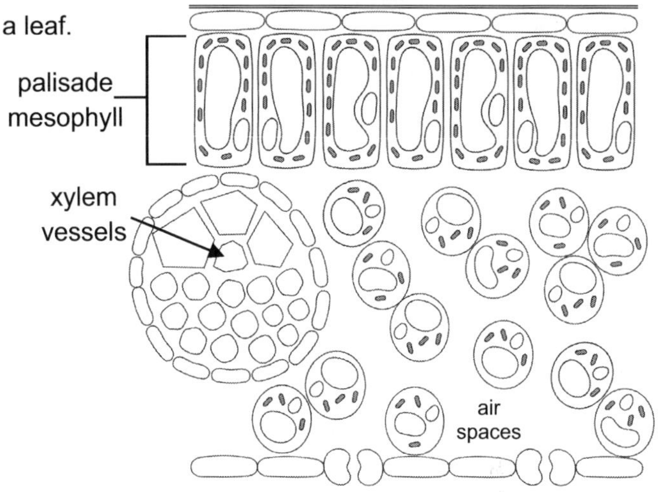


**a.** Draw arrows to show water vapour evaporating from the cells inside the leaf. Draw these arrows in blue.

**b.** Draw arrows to show water vapour diffusing through the air spaces in the spongy mesophyll. Draw these arrows in red.

**c.** Draw arrows to show water vapour diffusing out of the stomata. Draw these arrows in green.

**d.** Draw arrows to show water moving out of the xylem to replace the water that has been lost. Draw these arrows in black.

**3.** Describe what is meant by the transpiration stream.

**4.** Transpiration plays three main roles in the plant.

Complete the following paragraph using the words below.

**cooling** **water** **energy** **photosynthesis** **warm** **mineral**

The transpiration stream brings ____________ to the leaf. This is needed for the process of

____________________ . The water contains dissolved ________________ ions such as magnesium.

Magnesium ions are used by the plant to make chlorophyll. Finally, transpiration plays an important role

in ________________ the plant. When the water vapour evaporates from the leaf, this carries

away ________________ , which reduces the plant's temperature. This is especially important in

conditions where the weather is ________________ .

**5.** The rate of transpiration is increased by four different factors.

Complete each box to show how each factor increases the rate of transpiration.

| Higher temperatures | Dry conditions |
|---|---|
| | |

| Windy conditions | High light intensity |
|---|---|
| | |

**6.** The diagrams below show stomata in high light intensity and in hot conditions.

**a.** Label the diagrams to show the guard cells.

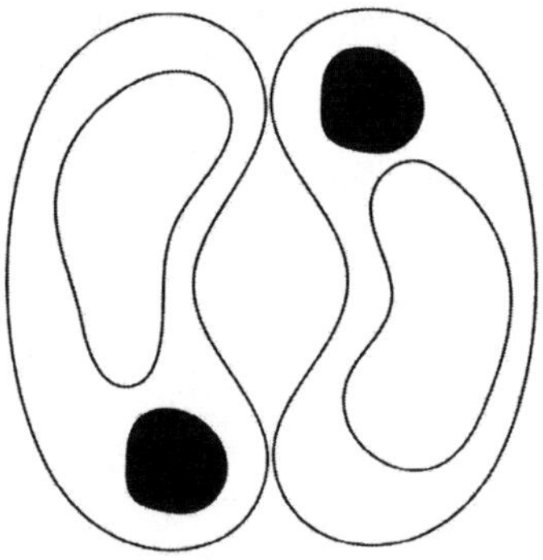

**High light intensity**

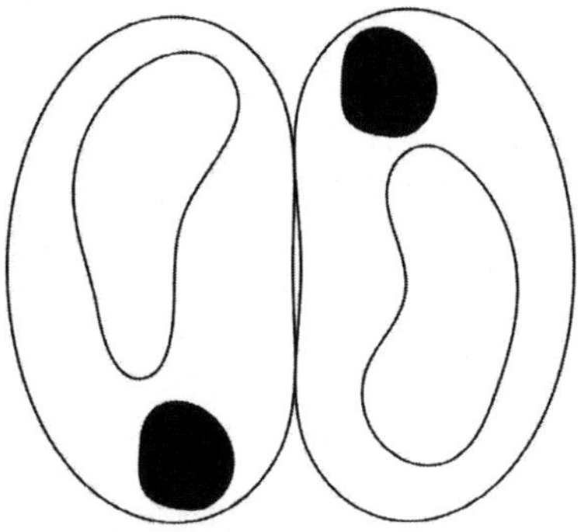

**Hot conditions**

**b.** Explain how the stomata open in conditions of high light intensity.

**c.** Stomata close in hot conditions. Explain why they do this and the effect of this on photosynthesis.

**d.** Plants in the desert often have fewer stomata than other plants. Suggest why.

# Chapter 3: Infection and Response

| |
|---|
| • Describe what is meant by communicable and non-communicable diseases. |
| • Describe the causes of different diseases and how diseases can interact. |
| • Describe what is meant by a pathogen and how their spread can be reduced. |
| • Calculate bacterial numbers and describe how bacteria can make us ill. |
| • Describe how viruses reproduce and how they can make us ill. |
| • Describe the causes, symptoms and treatments for the viral diseases measles and HIV. |
| • Describe the causes, symptoms and treatments for the bacterial diseases Salmonella and Gonorrhoea. |
| • Describe how Malaria can be transmitted and how transmission can be prevented. |
| • Describe the non-specific defence system in humans. |
| • Describe how the immune system protects us against pathogens. |
| • Describe the causes and symptoms of Tobacco Mosaic Virus and Rose Black Spot in plants. |
| • Describe how vaccination offers long-term protection against disease. |
| • Describe the role of antibiotics in treating bacterial diseases. |
| • Describe how medicines are tested including the ideas of a placebo and double-blind testing. |

# Communicable and Non-communicable Diseases

Exam tip: This topic is covered in both the Infection and Response part of the specification and also Organisation. It's really important to learn it.

**1.** Diseases can be caused by a range of different factors.

Complete the following paragraph using the words below.

**mental passed pathogens viruses measles heart disease stress pollution**

Good health involves a state of both physical and ________________ well being. Poor health can be caused by both communicable and non-communicable diseases. Communicable diseases can be ________________ from person to person via ________________ such as bacteria or ________________ . A good example of a communicable disease is ________________ .

Non-communicable diseases cannot be spread from person to person. A good example of a non-communicable disease is coronary ________________ . Poor health can also be caused by ________________, a poor diet or other factors eg ________________ .

**2.** Tick the correct boxes to show whether the diseases below are communicable or non-communicable.

| Disease | Communicable | Non-communicable |
|---|---|---|
| Measles | | |
| Cervical cancer | | |
| Human immunodeficiency virus (HIV) | | |
| Tuberculosis (TB) | | |
| Asthma | | |
| Depression | | |
| Human papilloma virus (HPV) | | |
| Dermatitis | | |
| Arthritis | | |
| Coronary heart disease | | |

**3.** Tuberculosis (TB) is a communicable lung disease caused by a bacterium.

**a.** Explain why most people who are exposed to the TB bacterium do not catch the disease.

**b.** Why are people with HIV more likely to catch TB than a person without HIV?

**4.** Sometimes one disease can be the cause of another disease.

Complete the sentences below by selecting the correct words from the boxes.

HPV is a relatively harmless communicable disease caused by a [fungus / virus / bacterium]. In women, infection with HPV can increase the risk of developing cancer of the [breast / ovaries / cervix].

**5.** Some diseases can be triggered by the immune system for example allergies.

**a.** Which of the following diseases are examples of allergies?

depression | asthma | dermatitis | measles

**b.** Describe how allergies can be triggered by the immune system.

**6.** Depression is an example of a mental illness.

**a.** Describe what is meant by a mental illness.

**b.** Arthritis is a physical illness as it affects the body.

People who develop arthritis can go on to develop depression.

Describe how arthritis can lead to depression.

# Pathogens

**1.** Many diseases are caused by pathogens.

**a.** Which of the boxes below shows the correct definition of a pathogen? Circle the correct box.

| A disease caused by the lack of a vitamin | A disease which can be spread from person to person | A microorganism that causes an infectious disease |
|---|---|---|

**b.** There are four common categories of pathogens. Write the four categories of pathogens below.

| | | | |
|---|---|---|---|

**c.** Under ideal conditions, bacteria can double in number every twenty minutes.

Imagine that a person gets a cut and 50 bacteria enter the person's bloodstream. Complete the table to show the number of bacteria present after less than five hours.

| Time (minutes) | Number of bacteria | Time (minutes) | Number of bacteria | Time (minutes) | Number of bacteria |
|---|---|---|---|---|---|
| 0 | 50 | 100 | | 200 | |
| 20 | 100 | 120 | | 220 | |
| 40 | | 140 | | 240 | |
| 60 | | 160 | | 260 | |
| 80 | | 180 | | 280 | |

**d.** When dealing with very large numbers such as those above, we often use standard form.

Circle the box which shows the correct version of standard form for the number of bacteria at 280 minutes.

Explain why the other two answers are incorrect.

| $81.92 \times 10^{4}$ | $8.192 \times 10^{5}$ | $8.192 \times 10^{-5}$ |
|---|---|---|

Explanation:

**e.** A short time after infection, the infected person can show symptoms of the illness.

Explain how bacteria make us feel ill.

**2.** Viruses are another type of pathogen.

**a.** What is the difference between bacteria and viruses in terms of their reproduction?

**b.** The diagrams below show the stages of a viral infection of a cell.

Describe what is happening in each stage of the process.

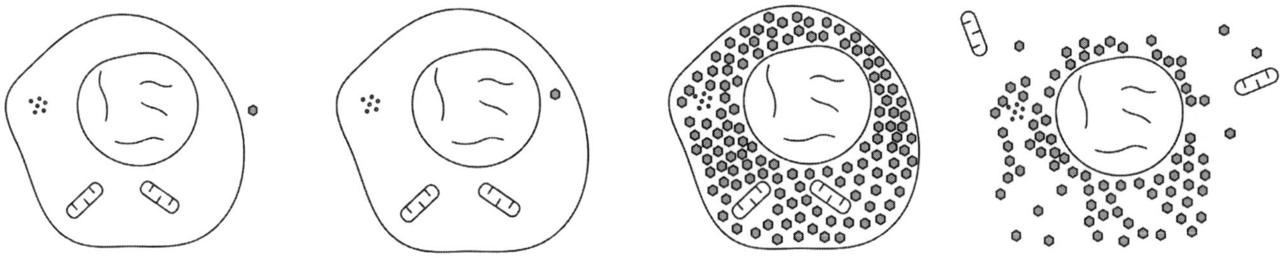

| Stage One | Stage Two | Stage Three |
|---|---|---|
| | | |

**c.** Use the stages above to explain how a viral infection makes us feel unwell.

**3.** Pathogens cause communicable diseases, in other words they can be spread from person to person.

**a.** Draw a line to connect each disease with how it is spread and how the spread can be prevented.

| | | |
|---|---|---|
| Human immunodeficiency virus (HIV) | Spread by drinking water containing sewage | Prevented by washing hands regularly |
| Influenza ('Flu) | Spread though sexual contact and sharing infected needles | Prevented by providing chlorinated drinking water to homes |
| Cholera | Spread by inhaling water droplets or touching infected surfaces | Prevented by using a condom during sexual intercourse |

**b.** How can we reduce the spread of highly infectious diseases such as Ebola virus?

**c.** How can we reduce the spread of pathogens for less infectious diseases eg Measles?

# Measles and HIV

**1.** Measles is a highly infectious disease caused by a virus.

**a.** Fill in the boxes to show the first two symptoms of measles.

| First symptom | Second symptom |
|---|---|
| | |

**b.** Describe how measles is spread from person to person.

**c.** In some cases, measles can be fatal. Circle two parts of the body which can be damaged by measles.

Digestive system | Heart | Breathing system | Brain | Immune system

**d.** Explain why measles is not a very common disease.

**2.** HIV is also caused by a virus.

**a.** Infection with HIV has several stages. Number the following stages in the correct order.

| Stage | Number |
|---|---|
| Patient may catch infectious disease eg TB or develop cancer | |
| A 'flu-like illness lasting one to two weeks | |
| Immune system becomes severely damaged | |
| Initial infection with HIV | |
| Virus attacks cells of the immune system | |
| Late state HIV / AIDS can be fatal | |

**b.** HIV can be controlled using antiretroviral drugs. Explain how these drugs work.

**c.** HIV is a communicable disease. Describe two ways that HIV can be transmitted.

**3.** Explain why neither measles nor HIV can be treated using antibiotics.

# Salmonella and Gonorrhoea

**1.** Unlike viruses, bacteria do not need to enter a host cell to reproduce.

State another difference between bacteria and viruses.

**2.** Salmonella food poisoning is a disease caused by bacteria.

**a.** Describe how a person becomes infected with salmonella food poisoning.

**b.** Circle the boxes below which show the symptoms of salmonella food poisoning.

| | | | | | |
|---|---|---|---|---|---|
| Fever | Pain when urinating | Vomiting | Sneezing | Diarrhoea | Abdominal cramps |

**c.** Describe how salmonella bacteria lead to these symptoms.

**d.** Explain why salmonella food poisoning is uncommon in the UK.

**3.** Gonorrhoea is a sexually-transmitted disease (STD) caused by a bacterium.

**a.** Describe the symptoms of gonorrhoea.

**b.** In the past, gonorrhoea was treated using the antibiotic penicillin.

Now gonorrhoea is treated with different antibiotics. Describe why.

**c.** Fill in the boxes to describe two ways to prevent the spread of gonorrhoea.

# Malaria

**1.** Malaria causes over 400 000 deaths every year around the world.

Complete the following paragraph using the words below.

**pathogen mosquitoes directly vector protist communicable uninfected**

Malaria is a ________________ disease caused by a ________________ . However, unlike many other diseases, malaria cannot be passed ________________ from person to person. Instead, the malaria pathogen is spread via ________________ . First the mosquito bites an infected person. Blood and the malaria ________________ pass into the mosquito. The mosquito then bites an ________________ person, passing on the pathogen. Because the mosquito carries the protist from one person to another, scientists call it a ________________ .

**2.** One way to prevent malaria is to stop the vector (mosquitoes) from breeding.

**a.** Describe where mosquitoes prefer to breed.

**b.** Fill in the boxes to show two ways to stop mosquitoes from breeding.

**c.** Suggest why these methods have not been fully successful in preventing malaria.

**d.** In many places where malaria is present, people sleep under mosquito nets.

Explain how mosquito nets can be used to reduce the spread of malaria.

# Non-specific Defence Systems

**1.** The skin forms the first barrier against the entry of pathogens.

Complete the sentences below by selecting the correct words from the boxes.

The skin prevents pathogens from entering the body in a number of ways. The outer part of the skin consists of a layer of [large / dead / living] skin cells. This is a thick barrier which is difficult for pathogens to penetrate. The skin is also covered in a layer of [mucus / acid / sebum] which can kill bacteria. If the skin is damaged then pathogens can enter. To prevent this, the damaged area rapidly forms a [scab / scar / plug] to block the entry of pathogens.

**2.** Pathogens can also enter our body when we breathe.

**a.** Which of the pathogens below can enter through our breathing system? Circle one box.

HIV | Salmonella | Malaria | Measles

**b.** Describe how the interior of the nose prevents the entry of pathogens.

**c.** The trachea and bronchi are covered with tiny hairs called cilia.

Label the trachea and bronchi on the diagram on the right.

**d.** Describe how the cilia prevent pathogens from making their way into the lungs.

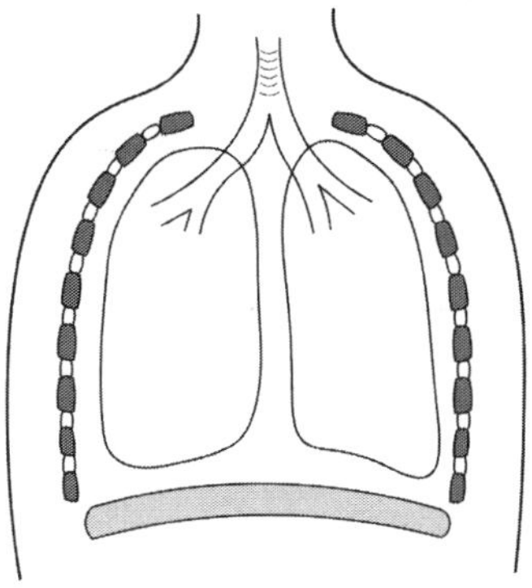

**3.** Pathogens can also enter our body on our food.

Describe how the stomach protects us from pathogens entering our digestive system.

# The Immune System

Exam tip: Remember to never say that white blood cells eat a pathogen. The correct term is "ingest" which means "take in".

**1.** In the bloodstream, pathogens can multiply rapidly and release toxins which make us feel ill.

White blood cells form the immune system and can ingest pathogens which have invaded the body.

**a.** Next to each of the diagrams, describe what is happening at each stage.

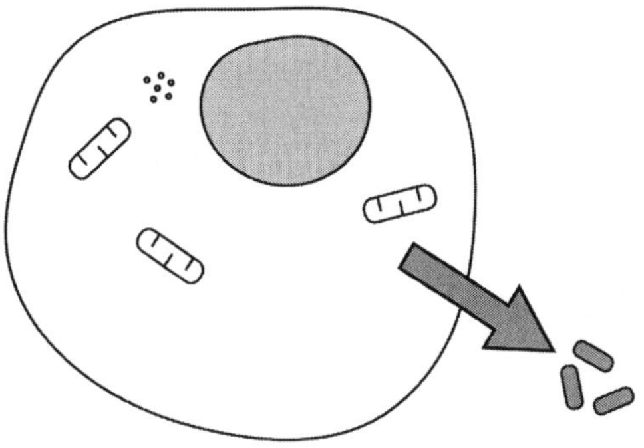

Stage One

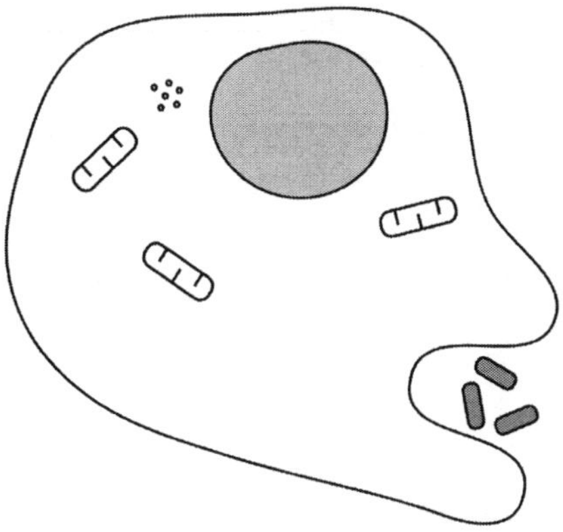

Stage Two

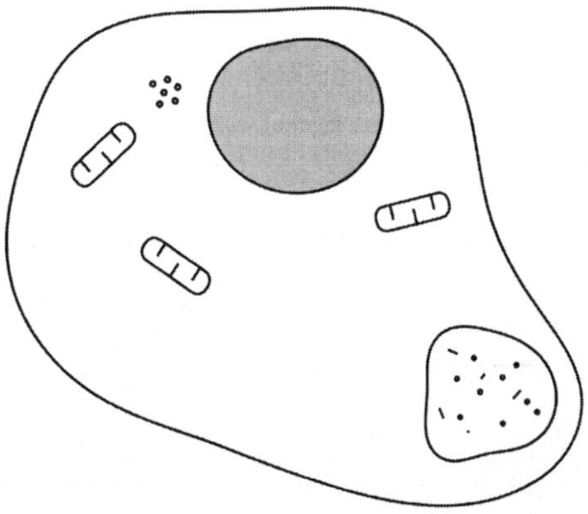

Stage Three

**b.** Which word do scientists use to describe the whole process shown above?

Lymphocytosis | Phagocytosis | Endocytosis

**2.** Some types of white blood cells can release antibodies. This is shown in the diagram below.

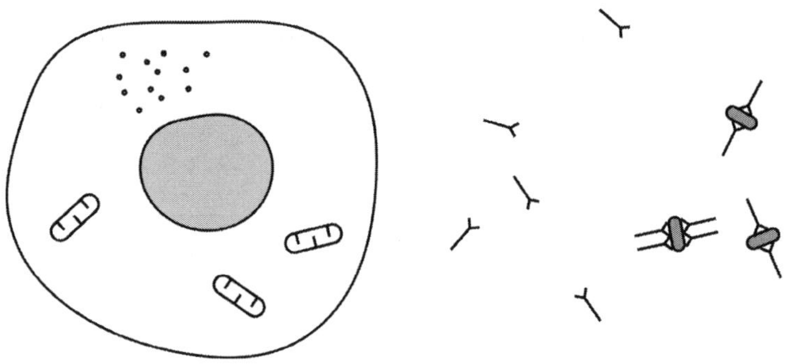

**a.** Label the diagram to show the white blood cells, antibodies and pathogens.

**b.** Use the diagram to describe how antibodies protect us from infection by pathogens.

**c.** Explain the following two facts:

- A person who has caught measles cannot catch measles again in their life.

- Catching measles does not protect us against other diseases such as HIV or influenza.

**d.** Suggest why this white blood cell contains a large number of ribosomes.

**3.** Some white blood cells produce antitoxins. This is shown below.

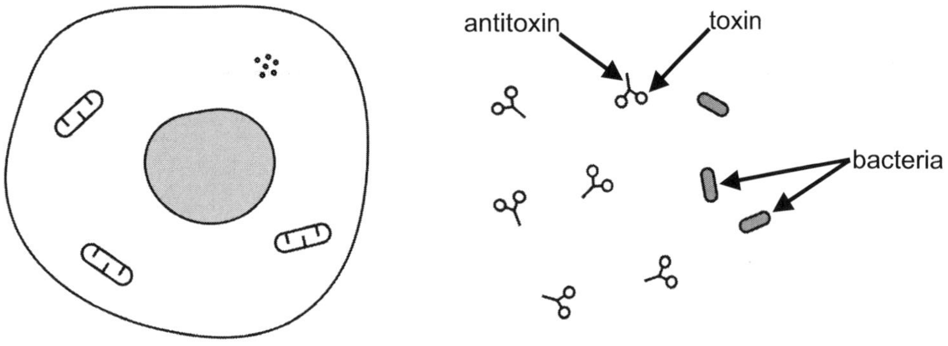


Describe how antitoxins protect us from the harmful effects of bacteria.

# Infectious Diseases in Plants

**1.** Plants are also exposed to pathogens. One of these is tobacco mosaic virus (TMV).

**a.** Which of the following are true about TMV? Circle the correct boxes.

| | | |
|---|---|---|
| TMV causes black spots on leaves | TMV causes patches of discolouration | TMV is caused by a fungus |
| TMV is caused by a virus | TMV only affects tobacco plants | TMV is not specific to one plant |

**b.** Explain why plants which are infected by TMV grow more slowly than uninfected plants.

**2.** Another plant pathogen causes the disease rose black spot.

Complete the following paragraph using the words below.

**fungus fungicides wind purple yellow slowly photosynthesis communicable destroying**

Rose black spot is a ____________________ plant disease which is caused by a ____________________

This is spread from plant to plant via water or the ____________________ . When a plant becomes infected, the leaves develop spots which are black or ____________________ . Eventually, infected leaves turn ____________________ and fall off the plant. This causes the plant to have a reduced rate of ____________________ . Because of this, plants which are infected with rose black spot will grow more ____________________ than plants which are not infected. We can treat infected plants by removing infected leaves and ____________________ them eg by burning. We can also spray the plant with ____________________ . These are chemicals which kill fungi.

# Vaccination

**1.** People in the UK receive a large number of vaccinations in their lifetime.

The diagram below shows what happens when a person receives a vaccination.

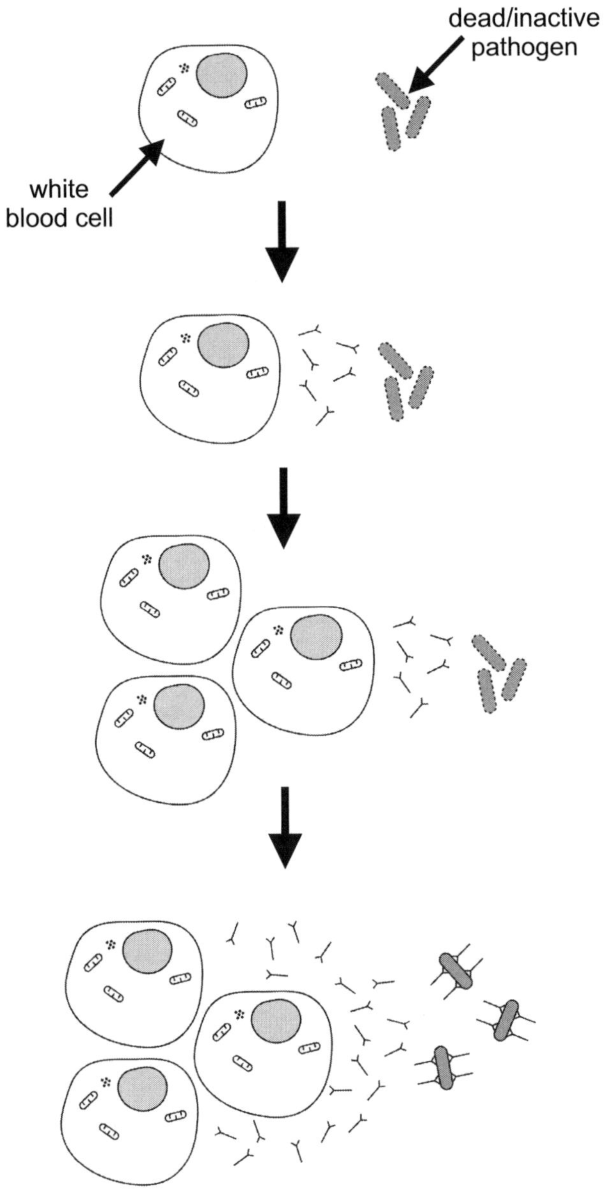


Stage One

Stage Two

Stage Three

Stage Four

**a.** Complete the diagram to show what is taking place at each stage. Use the boxes below.

| | | | |
|---|---|---|---|
| The white blood cells undergo mitosis to produce lots of identical copies | A small amount of dead or inactive pathogen is introduced into the body | If the pathogen enters the body, antibodies are rapidly produced, preventing infection | The white blood cells produce antibodies against the dead or inactive pathogen |

**b.** Explain why the pathogen used in a vaccination cannot give a person the actual disease.

**2.** The graph below shows the number of antibodies in a person's bloodstream after vaccination.

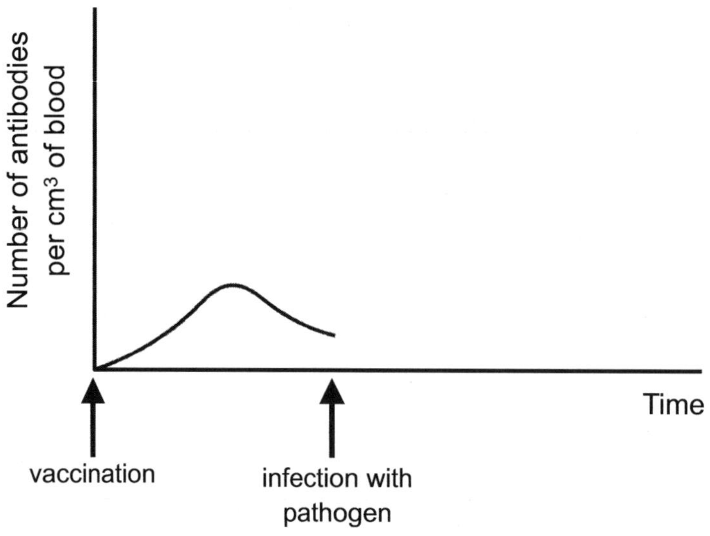


**a.** Complete the graph to show how the number of antibodies changes after the live pathogen enters the body.

**b.** Describe two differences in how the number of antibodies changes after vaccination and after the live pathogen enters the body.

**c.** Explain why the vaccination will not protect the person against infection with a different pathogen.

**3.** Vaccinating a whole population can also protect people who have not been vaccinated, for example a person who is new to a country.

**a.** The diagram shows a population where everyone has been vaccinated apart from one person. The unvaccinated person is shown circled.

Use the diagram to explain how the unvaccinated person will not get infected.

**b.** What name do scientists give to this kind of protection? Circle the correct box.

| | | |
|---|---|---|
| community immunity | group immunity | herd immunity |

# Antibiotics

Exam tip: We're going to see antibiotic resistance in more detail in Biology 2 when we look at evidence for evolution by natural selection.

**1.** In the past, bacterial pathogens have been a major cause of death and disease.

**a.** Circle the boxes below which show diseases caused by bacterial pathogens.

| | | | | | |
|---|---|---|---|---|---|
| Malaria | Gonorrhoea | HIV | Salmonella | Asthma | Measles |

**b.** Complete the sentences below by selecting the correct words from the boxes.

In the 1940s, antibiotics were discovered. The first antibiotic that was commonly used was [tetracycline. / penicillin. / cephalexin.]

Antibiotics kill [bacteria / fungi / viruses] inside the human body but they do not harm body cells. Over time, certain antibiotics were overused and stopped working. The bacteria had evolved and become [immune / resistive / resistant] to the antibiotic.

To avoid antibiotic resistance, doctors now use [multiple / specific / general] antibiotics for specific bacterial pathogens.

Doctors are also careful to never prescribe antibiotics for viral infections for example [measles. / salmonella. / gonorrhoea.]

**2.** Some bacterial diseases can be painful. Explain why doctors cannot prescribe just painkillers to treat these.

**3.** Many diseases are caused by viruses rather than bacteria.

Explain why it is difficult to develop drugs to treat diseases caused by viruses.

# Testing Medicines

**1.** In the past, lots of drugs were discovered in living organisms such as plants.

**a.** Draw a line to connect each drug to its function and then how it was discovered.

| | | |
|---|---|---|
| Digitalis | Painkiller | Extracted from penicillium mould |
| Aspirin | Antibiotic used to treat bacterial infections | Extracted from foxgloves |
| Penicillin | Used to treat heart conditions | Extracted from willow trees |

**b.** Which of the following scientists discovered penicillin?

| | | |
|---|---|---|
| Christiaan Barnard | Edward Jenner | Alexander Fleming |

**2.** Medicines have to undergo three tests. For each of the tests below, explain what is being investigated.

- Toxicity
- Effectiveness
- Dosage

**3.** New medicines first undergo preclinical testing.

**a.** What are the new medicines tested on at this stage?

**b.** Explain why drugs are not first tested on humans.

**4.** Once the drug has passed pre-clinical testing, it is given to humans. This is called clinical testing.

**a.** In the first stage, a very low dose of the drug is given to healthy volunteers.

Explain why only a very low dose of the drug is used at this stage.

**b.** In the second stage, testing continues in order to find the optimal dose.

What is meant by the words "optimal dose"?

**5.** Modern drug tests are always double-blind and involve using a placebo.

**a.** Which of the following best describes what is meant by a placebo?

| | | |
|---|---|---|
| The placebo is the active drug but in a very low dose | The placebo looks like the treatment but contains no drug | The placebo is a drink of water containing no drug |

**b.** Explain the purpose of the placebo.

**c.** Complete the following paragraph using the words below.

**doctors** **drug** **active** **bias** **placebo**

In a double-blind trial, one group receives the ____________________ drug and another group receives the ____________________ . The placebo looks exactly like the treatment but does not contain any active ____________________ . Neither the patient nor the ____________________ know who is receiving the drug or the placebo. This is to prevent ____________________ for example if the doctors gave more attention to patients that they knew were receiving the active drug.

# Chapter 4: Bioenergetics

| |
|---|
| • State the word equation for photosynthesis. |
| • Recognise the chemical formulas of the reactants and products in photosynthesis. |
| • Describe what is meant by a limiting factor, giving examples. |
| • Identify limiting factors from graphs showing rate of photosynthesis. |
| • Explain how temperature can affect the rate of photosynthesis. |
| • Describe how plants use the glucose produced in photosynthesis. |
| • Describe how to measure the effect of light intensity on the rate of photosynthesis (required practical). |
| • Describe what is meant by the inverse-square law and how this relates to the effect of light intensity on the rate of photosynthesis. |
| • Describe how the idea of limiting factors can be used to determine the optimum conditions for plant growth in greenhouses. |
| • State the word equation for respiration. |
| • Recognise the chemical formulas of the reactants and products in respiration. |
| • State the uses of the energy released during respiration. |
| • Describe the differences between aerobic and anaerobic respiration. |
| • Describe the changes that take place in the body during and after exercise. |
| • Describe what is meant by the oxygen debt. |
| • Describe what is meant by metabolism and give examples of metabolic reactions. |

# Photosynthesis

Exam tip: Make certain that you learn the word equation for photosynthesis.
Remember that you do not need to learn the balanced symbol equation.

**1.** Complete the sentences by selecting the correct words from the boxes.

Plants use light as their source of [nutrients / elements / energy]. To trap the light, plants carry out the process of [metabolism / photosynthesis / respiration]. Because this takes in light energy, it is [an endothermic / an exothermic / a reversible] reaction. Photosynthesis takes place in the leaves of the plant. These contain [enzymes / chlorophyll / ribosomes] which can absorb light energy.

**2.** The word equation for photosynthesis shows us the chemicals involved.

**a.** Complete the word equation by selecting the correct chemical from each box.

[water / oxygen / glucose / carbon dioxide] + [water / oxygen / glucose / carbon dioxide] —light / chlorophyll→ [water / oxygen / glucose / carbon dioxide] + [water / oxygen / glucose / carbon dioxide]

**b.** Draw a line from the chemical to the correct formula.

| Chemical | Formula |
| --- | --- |
| carbon dioxide | $C_6H_{12}O_6$ |
| water | $O_2$ |
| glucose | $CO_2$ |
| oxygen | $H_2O$ |

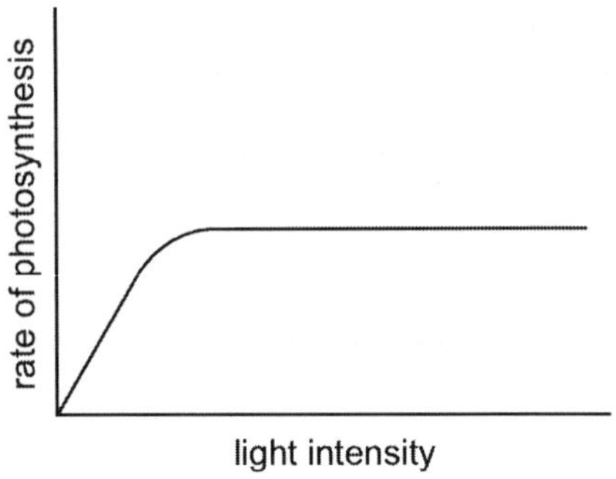


**3.** The graph on the left shows how the rate of photosynthesis changes when we increase the light intensity.

**a.** What happens to the rate of photosynthesis when we initially increase the light intensity? Explain your answer.

**b.** Mark on the graph the point where light intensity is a limiting factor and explain what is meant by the term limiting factor.

**c.** Mark on the graph the point where light intensity is no longer a limiting factor.

**d.** We get a similar graph if we vary the level of carbon dioxide. This is shown on the right.

Mark on the graph where carbon dioxide is the limiting factor.

**e.** When the graph levels off, some other factor is limiting. Suggest what this other factor could be.

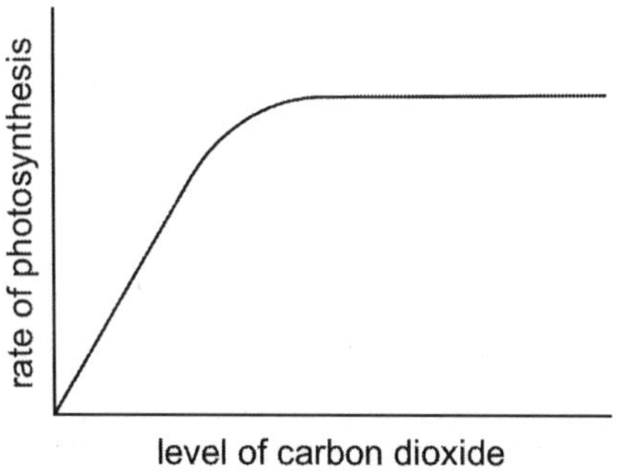


**f.** Variegated plants have leaves with patches of chlorophyll. Explain why these plants may have a lower rate of photosynthesis compared to a plant with non-variegated leaves.

**4.** The graph below shows the effect of increasing the temperature on the rate of photosynthesis.

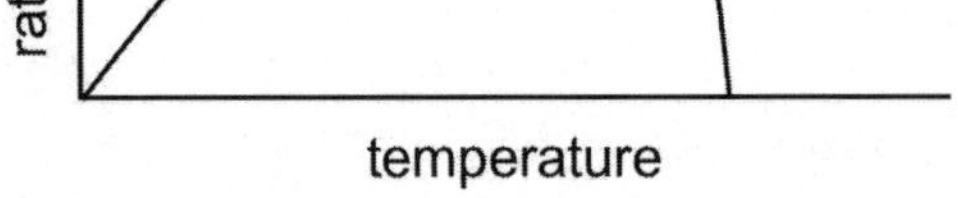


**a.** Explain why the rate of photosynthesis increases as we initially increase the temperature.

**b.** If the temperature is too high then the enzymes denature and the rate of photosynthesis sharply decreases.

Mark on the graph the point where the enzymes denature.

**c.** Which of the following best describes what happens to an enzyme when it denatures?

| | | |
|---|---|---|
| The substrate molecule vibrates. The substrate changes shape and no longer fits the active site. | The enzyme molecule vibrates. The active site changes shape and no longer fits the substrate. | The amino acids which form the enzyme are destroyed as the temperature increases. |

# Uses of Glucose from Photosynthesis

**1.** The glucose produced in photosynthesis can be used in respiration.

**a.** Read the statements below and circle the statements that are true.

| | | |
|---|---|---|
| Respiration is used by the cell to release the energy stored in glucose | Respiration takes place in the chloroplasts | Respiration only occurs during night time when the plant cannot photosynthesise |
| Respiration takes place in the mitochondria | Respiration takes place all the time | Photosynthesis can only take place during the day time when it is light |

**b.** Explain why plants also need to store some of the glucose produced in photosynthesis as starch.

**2.** In many plants, some of the glucose produced by photosynthesis is converted to fats and oils.

What is the purpose of the fats and oils produced by plants in this way?

**3.** The diagram on the right shows a typical plant cell found in a leaf.

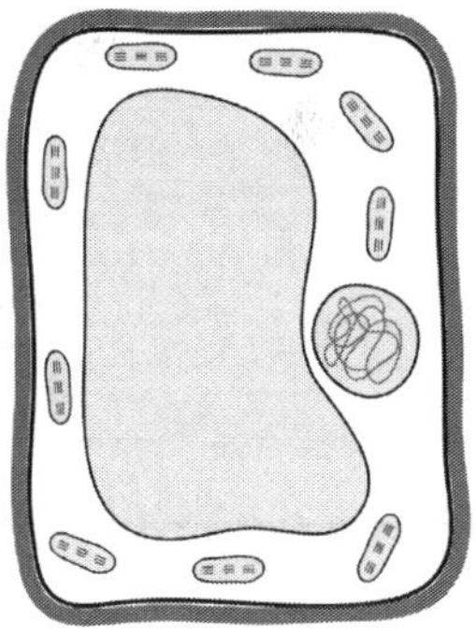

**a.** Some of the glucose produced in photosynthesis is used to make the molecule cellulose.

Circle the part of the plant cell which is made from cellulose.

| | | |
|---|---|---|
| cell membrane | vacuole | cell wall |

**b.** Label this on the diagram.

**4.** Some of the glucose produced by photosynthesis is used by the plant to make amino acids.

**a.** Which molecules are made by joining together amino acids?

**b.** Give the name of the ion which plants absorb from the soil to make amino acids from glucose.

# Required Practical: Photosynthesis

Exam tip: With any required practical, try to learn the sequence of steps.
Remember to link any step with the equipment needed for that step.

**1.** We start by placing a boiling tube 10 cm from an LED light source.

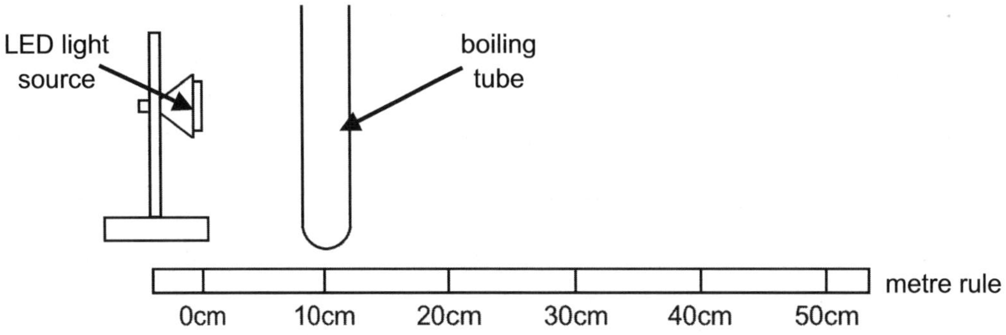


Explain the advantage of using an LED light source rather than a normal light bulb.

**2.** Now we fill the boiling tube with a solution of sodium hydrogen carbonate and place a piece of pondweed into the solution.

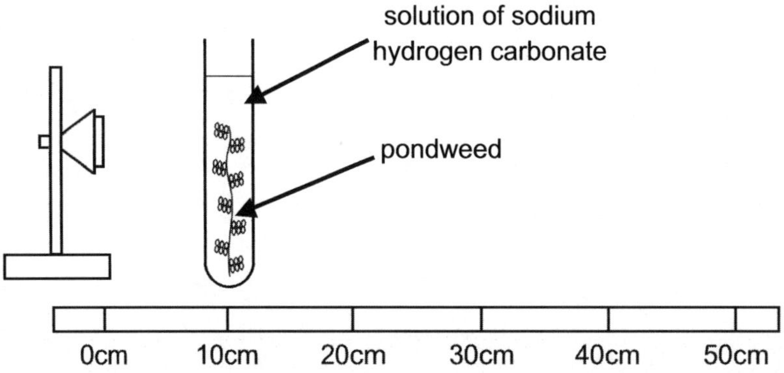


**a.** Explain why we use a solution of sodium hydrogen carbonate rather than simply water.

**b.** Why is it important that we place the pondweed with the cut side at the top?

**c.** We now leave the pondweed for five minutes. Why is this important?

**3.** Bubbles will now start to be produced from the cut end of the pondweed.

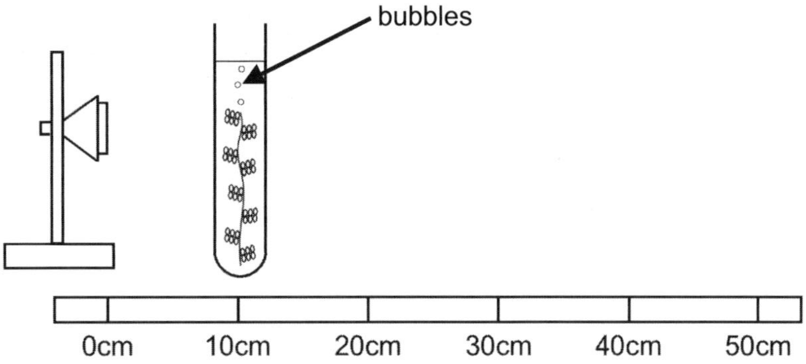


**a.** What is this gas and how is it produced?

**b.** We now start a stopwatch and count the number of bubbles produced in one minute.

We then repeat the experiment two more times and calculate a mean value.

A student's results are shown below.

| Distance of pondweed from lamp (cm) | Number of bubbles produced in one minute | | | |
|---|---|---|---|---|
| | Repeat 1 | Repeat 2 | Repeat 3 | Mean |
| 10 | 36 | 40 | 12 | |

The results show an anomalous result. Identify the anomalous result in the table.

**c.** Calculate the mean value and write this in the table.

We now repeat the whole experiment increasing the distance to 20 cm, 30 cm, 40 cm and 50 cm.

**4.** Some of the variables in this experiment are shown below.

Write **IV** next to the independent variable, **DV** next to the dependent variable and **CV** next to the control variables.

| Variable | Type of variable | Reason for answer |
|---|---|---|
| The species of pondweed | | |
| The concentration of sodium hydrogen carbonate solution | | |
| The volume of sodium hydrogen carbonate solution | | |
| The distance between the LED light and the pondweed | | |
| The LED light source | | |
| The temperature of the room | | |
| The number of bubbles produced per minute | | |

**5.** There are two problems with the method outlined above.

**a.** Describe the two problems in the spaces below.

| **Problem 1** | **Problem 2** |
|---|---|
| | |

**b.** We can address these problems by using the apparatus below.

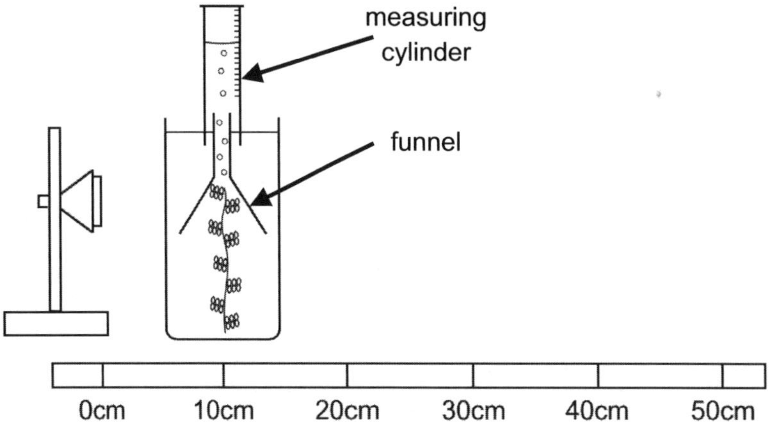


Explain how this is a more accurate way of measuring the rate of photosynthesis than the previous method.

**6.** The graph shows how the number of bubbles per minutes varies with the distance from the light source.

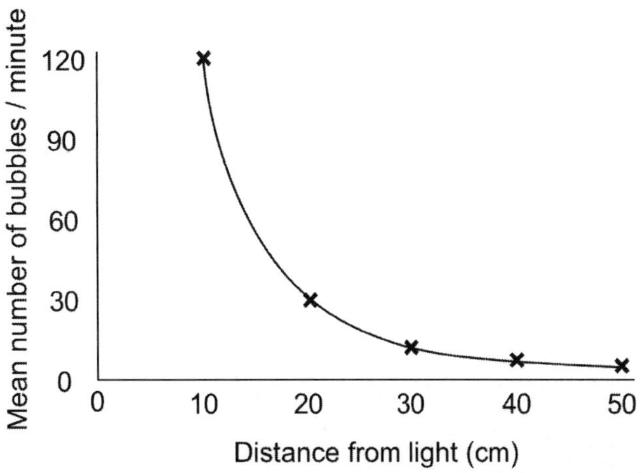


**a.** Use the graph to determine the mean number of bubbles per minute at the following distances.

| Distance (cm) | Mean number of bubbles per minute |
|---|---|
| 10 | |
| 20 | |
| 40 | |

**b.** These results follow the inverse-square law. How do the data show that?

**c.** Explain these results in terms of light intensity and photosynthesis.

# Limiting Factors

**1.** We started looking at limiting factors in the chapter on photosynthesis.

The graph shows the effect of changing light intensity on the rate of photosynthesis.

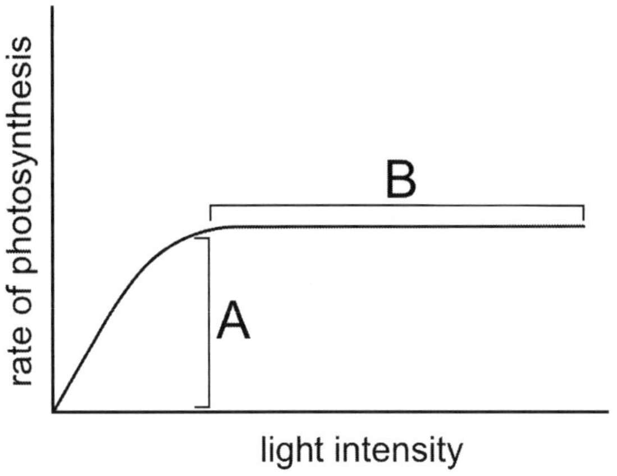


**a.** Which part of the graph shows where light intensity is a limiting factor? Explain your answer.

**b.** Which part of the graph shows where light intensity is not a limiting factor? Explain how the graph shows this.

**c.** State the factors that could be limiting the rate of photosynthesis when light intensity is <u>not limiting</u>.

The graph below shows the same experiment but with the concentration of carbon dioxide increased.

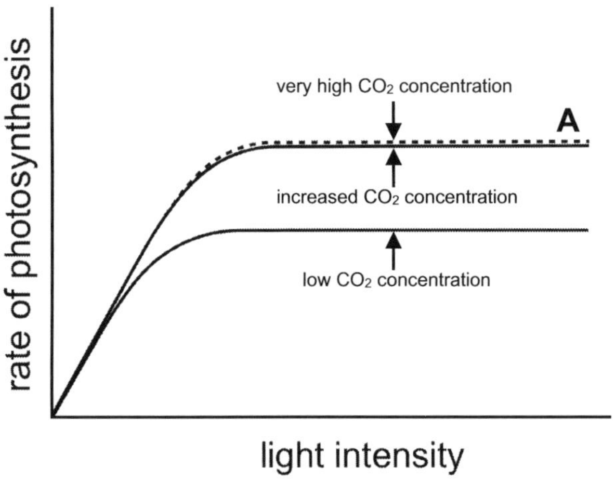


**d.** Explain how this graph shows that carbon dioxide was the limiting factor at high light intensity.

**e.** Explain how the graph shows that carbon dioxide was not the liming factor at point A.

**f.** It is possible that at very high concentrations of carbon dioxide, the temperature is now the limiting factor.

Describe how we could investigate whether this is the case.

**g.** Many gardeners grow crops in greenhouses. The greenhouses often contain oil burners.

Describe the benefit of using oil burners in greenhouses.

**h.** Burning oil in greenhouses has to have economic benefits. What does this mean?

# Respiration

**1.** Energy is very important for all living organisms.

Complete the following paragraph using the words below.

**exothermic** **protein** **warm** **respiration** **movement** **chemical reactions** **amino acids**

Living organisms need energy for three main functions. Animals need energy for ________________ .

Mammals such as humans need energy in order to keep their bodies ____________ . All organisms

need energy for the ________________ which are used to build larger molecules from small ones.

For example, it takes energy to build ________________ molecules from ________________ .

Energy is released continually in all living organisms by the process of cellular ________________ .

Because respiration releases energy, it is an ________________ reaction.

**2.** The word equation for aerobic respiration is shown below.

**a.** Complete the equation by selecting the correct chemical from each box.

| water / oxygen / glucose / carbon dioxide | + | water / oxygen / glucose / carbon dioxide | → | water / oxygen / glucose / carbon dioxide | + | water / oxygen / glucose / carbon dioxide |
|---|---|---|---|---|---|---|

→ energy

**b.** We saw the chemical symbols for these molecules in the section on photosynthesis.

Write the correct chemical symbol under each chemical.

| glucose | oxygen | carbon dioxide | water |
|---|---|---|---|
| ↓ | ↓ | ↓ | ↓ |
| | | | |

**c.** Explain why aerobic respiration releases a great deal of energy.

**3.** Under certain conditions, muscle cells cannot get the oxygen that they need for aerobic respiration.

**a.** Why do muscle cells need a great deal of oxygen? Circle the correct box.

| To digest food molecules | For contraction eg during exercise | To release hormones |
|---|---|---|

**b.** The diagram below shows the equation for anaerobic respiration.

Complete the diagram to show the missing products.

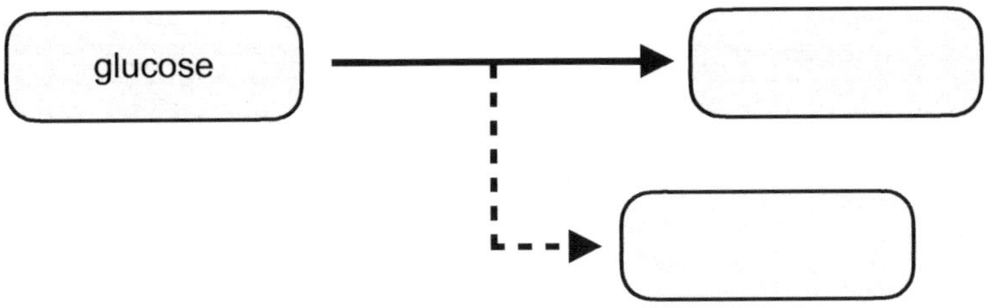


**c.** In terms of the molecules required, how is anaerobic respiration different to aerobic respiration?

**d.** Explain why anaerobic respiration releases much less energy than aerobic respiration.

**4.** Anaerobic respiration can also take place in plant cells and in yeast cells.

**a.** Complete the diagram to show the missing products.

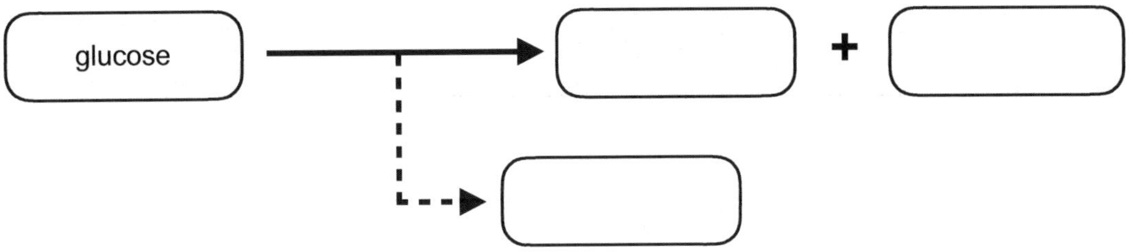


**b.** Anaerobic respiration in yeast cells is also called fermentation.

Explain how fermentation in yeast is useful in bread making and in making beer.

| Bread making | Making beer |
|---|---|
| | |

# Exercise

**1.** The energy demands of the body change when we are exercising.

Complete the sentences by selecting the correct words from the boxes.

During exercise, the body needs more energy. To provide this, the rate of aerobic respiration [stays the same. / increases. / decreases.]

Now, body cells require [less / the same / more] oxygen. To provide this, both the breathing rate and the breathing volume also [stay the same. / increase. / decrease.] This means that we take deeper breaths and more breaths per minute. The heart rate also increases so that the oxygenated blood can be delivered more efficiently to the [brain / muscle / stomach] cells.

**2.** During exercise, anaerobic respiration can also take place. This is shown in the diagram below.

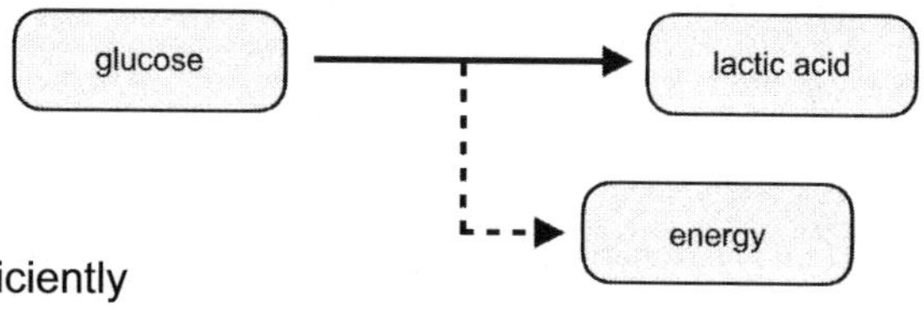


**a.** Explain why the body now carries out anaerobic respiration.

**b.** Use the diagram to explain why muscle cells stop contracting efficiently during intense exercise.

**c.** The lactic acid is taken from the muscle cells into the bloodstream.

Which organ is the lactic acid taken to (circle the correct answer)?

brain | stomach | pancreas | liver

**d.** The lactic acid is now converted back to glucose. This is shown in the diagram below.

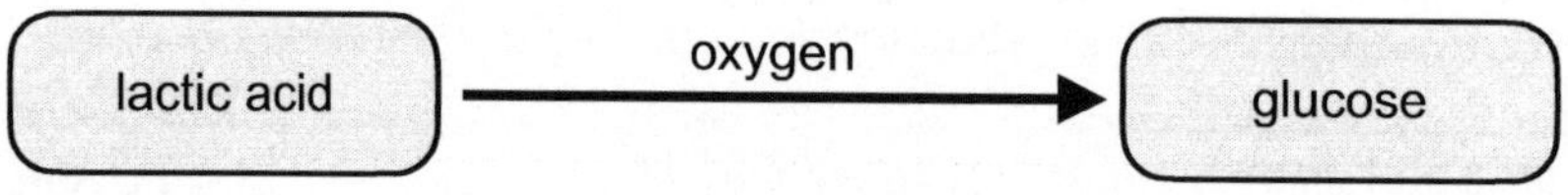


Use the diagram and the idea of the oxygen debt to explain why people continue breathing rapidly even after they have finished exercising.

# Metabolism

**1.** Which of the following is the correct definition of metabolism?

| | | | |
|---|---|---|---|
| Reactions which require energy | Reactions which form large molecules | All the chemical reactions in a cell or the body | Reactions which release energy |

**2.** As we saw in a previous chapter, plants make the sugar glucose by photosynthesis.

The glucose is then converted into other molecules.

**a.** Complete the diagram below to show the functions of the molecules produced from glucose.

Glucose in plants

→ Cellulose

→ Starch

→ Amino acids

**b.** Which mineral ion do plants need to make amino acids from glucose?

**3.** There are thousands of metabolic reactions in animals such as humans.

**a.** Glucose is used in respiration but it can also be stored.

State the name of the glucose storage molecule in animals.

**b.** Lipids (fats) play an important role in cells.

Complete the diagram to show how lipids are produced.

1 molecule of + 3 molecules of → 1 molecule of lipid

**c.** In which part of the cell are lipids found?

**d.** Excess proteins are also broken down in metabolic reactions.

Select the correct words to complete the sentence below.

Excess proteins are broken down to ______________ which is excreted by the ______________

**liver** **amino acids** **uric acid** **kidneys** **urea**

# Biology Paper 1
# Combined Science (Higher)

## GCSE Specimen Paper

## Time allowed: 75 minutes

## Maximum marks: 70

Please note that this is a specimen exam paper written by freesciencelessons. The questions are meant to reflect the style of questions that you might see in your GCSE Biology exam.

Neither the exam paper nor the mark scheme have been endorsed by any exam board. The answers are my best estimates of what would be accepted but I cannot guarantee that this would be the case. I do not offer any guarantee that the level you achieve in this specimen paper is the level that you will achieve in the real exam.

**1** Lung cancer is a non-communicable disease.

**1 . 1** State what is meant by a non-communicable disease. **1 mark**

______________________________________________

______________________________________________

**Table 1** shows how the incidence of lung cancer in men in the UK has changed since 1995.

**Table 1**

| Year | Incidence of lung cancer in men per 100 000 people |
|---|---|
| 1995 | 132 |
| 2000 | 115 |
| 2005 | 104 |
| 2010 | 99 |
| 2015 | 92 |

The data above are shown in graphical form in **Figure 1**.

**Figure 1**

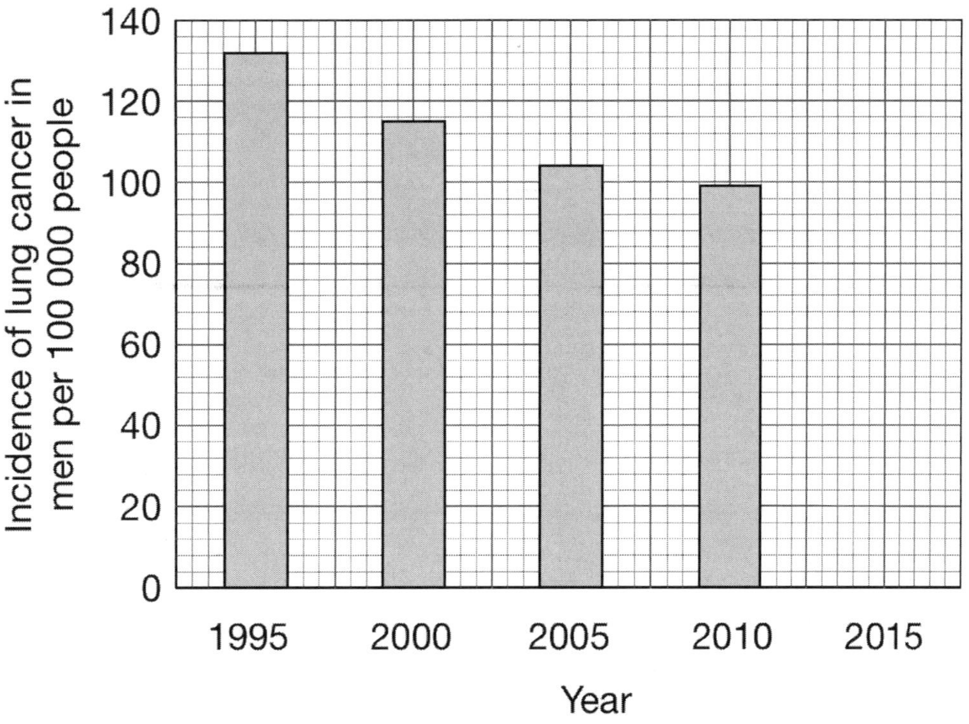

**1 . 2** Complete **Figure 1** to show the data for 2015.

**1 mark**

**1 . 3** A student made the following statement:

"The data show that the incidence of lung cancer is falling."

Give one reason why this is **not** supported by the data in **Figure 1**.

**1 mark**

______________________________________________________________

______________________________________________________________

To try to identify the cause of lung cancer, scientists carried out sampling.

The scientists asked a number of people about their smoking habits.

This produced a scattergraph similar to that shown in **Figure 2**.

**Figure 2**

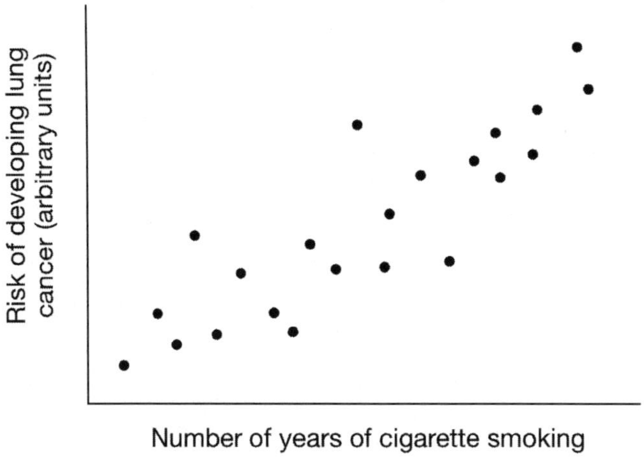


**1 . 4** Explain how the scattergraph in **Figure 2** suggests that the risk of developing lung cancer is correlated to the number of years a person smokes cigarettes.

**1 mark**

______________________________________________________________

______________________________________________________________

**1 . 5** Explain how the data do not prove that smoking cigarettes causes lung cancer.

**1 mark**

______________________________________________________________

______________________________________________________________

**1 . 6** Why is it important that sampling involves a very large number of people?

**1 mark**

______________________________________________________________________

______________________________________________________________________

**1 . 7** Scientists have identified a number of chemicals in cigarette smoke which can increase the risk of developing cancer.

What name do scientists give to chemicals such as these?

**1 mark**

______________________________________________________________________

**1 . 8** Describe the stages in the formation of a cancer in humans.

**4 marks**

______________________________________________________________________

______________________________________________________________________

______________________________________________________________________

______________________________________________________________________

______________________________________________________________________

______________________________________________________________________

______________________________________________________________________

______________________________________________________________________

**Total = 11**

**2** **Figure 3** shows a bacterial cell and a virus.

**Figure 3**

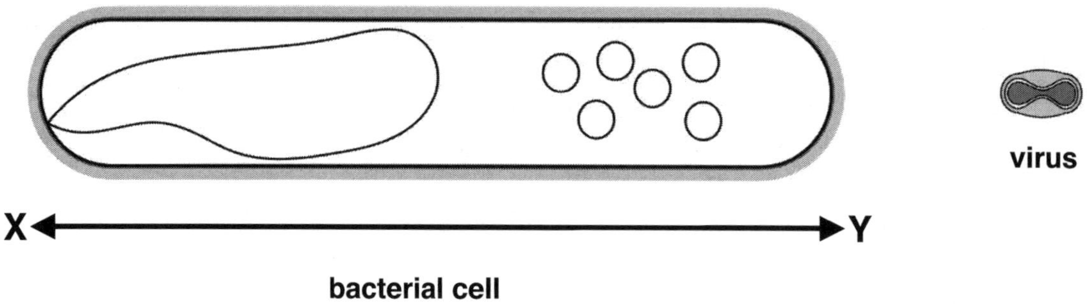


**2 . 1** The real length of the bacterial cell from X to Y is 0.002 mm.

Calculate the magnification used to produce the image.

Use the equation:

$$\text{magnification} = \frac{\text{size of image}}{\text{size of real object}}$$

**3 marks**

**2 . 2** An electron microscope has a higher magnification than a light microscope.

**1 mark**

State another advantage of an electron microscope over a light microscope.

**2 . 3** What is the real length of the virus? Show your working.

**2 marks**

Real length of virus = ________________ mm

**2 . 4** Explain why it is difficult to develop drugs which kill viruses.

**2 marks**

______________________________________________________________________

______________________________________________________________________

______________________________________________________________________

______________________________________________________________________

______________________________________________________________________

**2 . 5** HIV is a virus which can infect humans.

Describe the effect of HIV infection on a human.

Assume that the patient is **not** receiving antiretroviral drugs.

**3 marks**

______________________________________________________________________

______________________________________________________________________

______________________________________________________________________

______________________________________________________________________

______________________________________________________________________

______________________________________________________________________

______________________________________________________________________

______________________________________________________________________

**Total = 11**

**3** The word equation for photosynthesis is shown below.

carbon dioxide + water → glucose + oxygen

**3 . 1** Which of the following is the correct formula for glucose? Tick one box only.

**1 mark**

☐ $C_6H_{12}O_{12}$ ☐ $C_6H_{12}O_6$ ☐ $C_{12}H_{12}O_6$

**3 . 2** Explain why photosynthesis is an endothermic reaction.

**3 marks**

______________________________________________

______________________________________________

______________________________________________

______________________________________________

A scientist measured the effect of light intensity on the rate of photosynthesis of lettuce plants.

The results are shown in **Figure 4.**

**Figure 4**

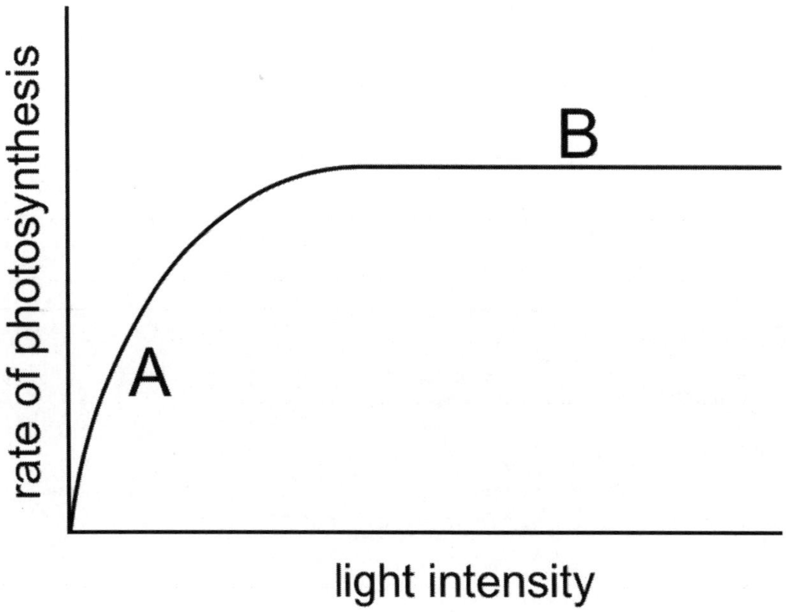

**3 . 3** Use the graph shown in **Figure 5** to explain how we know the following:

**2 marks**

At point A on the graph, light intensity is the limiting factor.

______________________________________________________________________

______________________________________________________________________

At point B on the graph, light intensity is not the limiting factor.

______________________________________________________________________

______________________________________________________________________

The scientist repeated the experiment using a higher concentration of carbon dioxide. The results are shown in **Figure 5**.

**Figure 5**

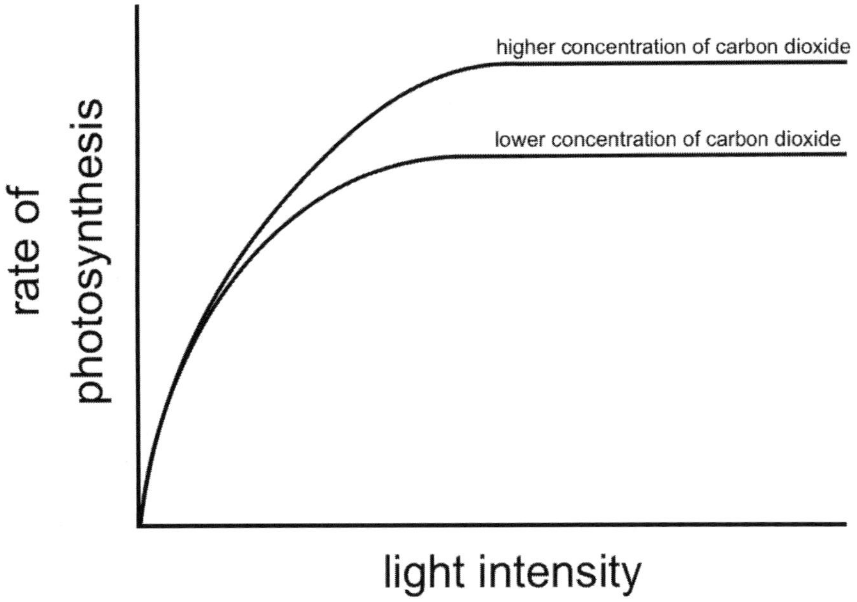


**3 . 4** State what the scientist can conclude from this experiment and explain your answer.

**2 marks**

______________________________________________________________________

______________________________________________________________________

______________________________________________________________________

______________________________________________________________________

**3 . 5** Lettuces are often grown in large greenhouses.

A farmer was keen to increase the yield of lettuces while still making a profit on the lettuces sold.

The farmer increased the concentration of carbon dioxide in the greenhouse and measured the yield of lettuce. The results are shown in **Figure 6**.

**Figure 6**

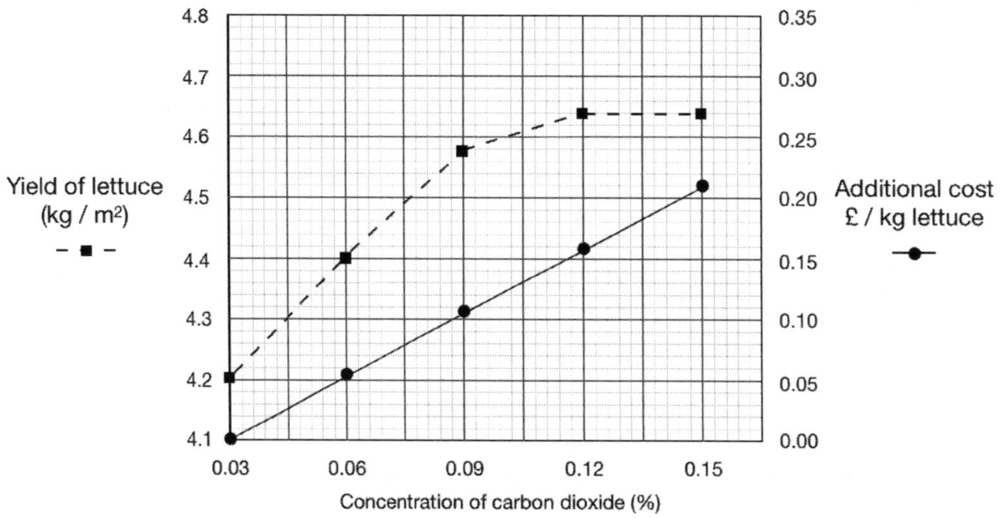


What advice would you give the farmer on the conditions in the greenhouse?

You should use data from **Figure 6** to support your answer.

**5 marks**

**Total = 13**

**4** Enzymes are used in the digestive system.

**4 . 1** Explain the purpose of enzymes in the digestive system.

**2 marks**

_______________________________________________

_______________________________________________

_______________________________________________

_______________________________________________

_______________________________________________

Amylase is an enzyme which breaks down the carbohydrate starch.

**4 . 2** State a location of amylase in the human digestive system.

**1 mark**

_______________________________________________

**4 . 3** Which molecule is produced when starch is digested by amylase?

Tick one box only.

**1 mark**

☐ glycerol ☐ amino acids ☐ simple sugars

**Question 4 continues on the next page**

**4 . 4** There are several models to explain how enzymes work.

One is called the **lock and key theory** and another is called the **induced fit model**.

These are shown in **Figure 7**.

**Figure 7**

**The Lock and Key Theory**

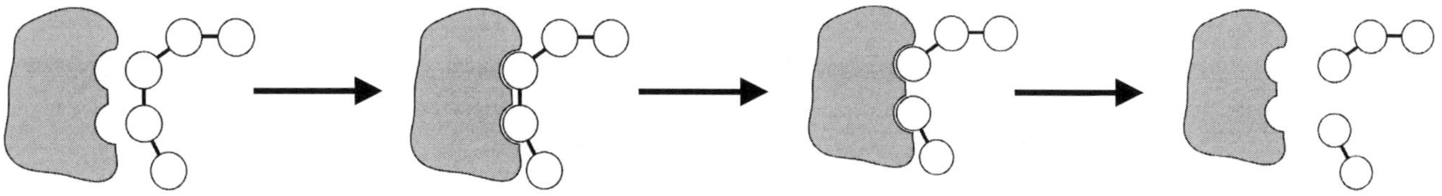

**The Induced Fit Model**

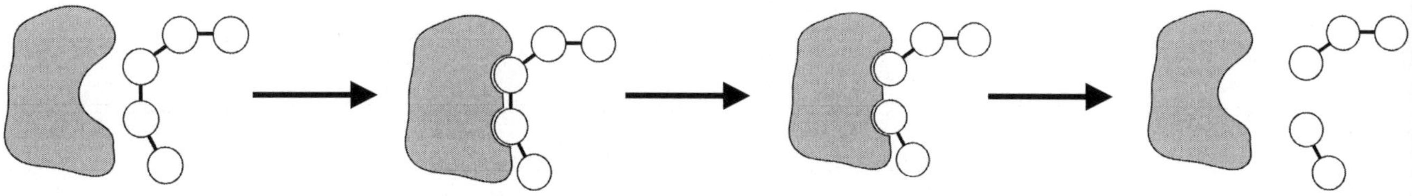

Use **Figure 7** to describe the similarities and differences between the two theories on enzyme action.

**3 marks**

A student decided to investigate the effect of pH on the enzyme amylase.

The student had access to the following:

- Starch solution
- Amylase solution
- A range of different pH buffers
- Iodine solution
- Standard laboratory equipment

**4 . 5** Describe how the student could carry out the investigation.

**6 marks**

The student then decided to investigate the effect of pH on the enzyme protease.

**4 . 6** Describe how the student could test for the presence of protein.

You should state the reagent used and the colour change if protein is present.

**2 marks**

Reagent ______________________________

Colour change if protein present ______________________________

______________________________

**4 . 7** The student's results are shown in **Table 2**.

**Table 2**

| pH | Time taken to digest protein (s) |
|---|---|
| 2 | 35 |
| 5 | 176 |
| 7 | 298 |
| 9 | no reaction |
| 11 | no reaction |

Use the data in **Table 2** to suggest the most likely location of this protease enzyme in the digestive system.

**3 marks**

______________________________

______________________________

______________________________

______________________________

______________________________

______________________________

**Total = 18**

**5** Humans have a double circulatory system.

**5 . 1** What is meant by a double circulatory system?

**3 marks**

______________________________________________

______________________________________________

______________________________________________

______________________________________________

______________________________________________

**Figure 8** shows a simplified diagram of the human heart.

**Figure 8**

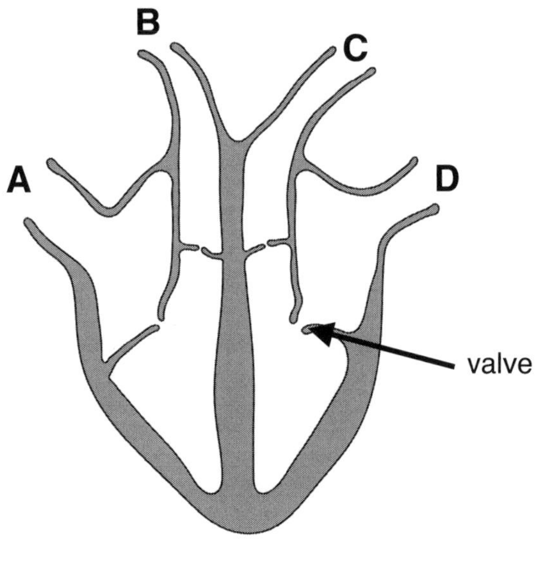


**5 . 2** Give the letters from the diagram of the following blood vessels.

**3 marks**

A blood vessel carrying blood to the lungs ☐

A blood vessel carrying blood to the body ☐

The vena cava ☐

**5 . 3** Describe the function of the valve shown in **Figure 8**.

**1 mark**

______________________________________________

______________________________________________

______________________________________________

**5 . 4** Some people experience a defective heart valve.

The defective heart valve can be replaced with a mechanical valve or a valve from an animal (a "biological valve").

State a disadvantage of these types of heart valve.

**2 marks**

Mechanical valve

______________________________________________

______________________________________________

Biological valve

______________________________________________

______________________________________________

**Question 5 continues on the next page**

Coronary heart disease is common in the Western world.

In coronary heart disease, layers of fatty material build up in the coronary artery.

This is shown in **Figure 9**.

**Figure 9**

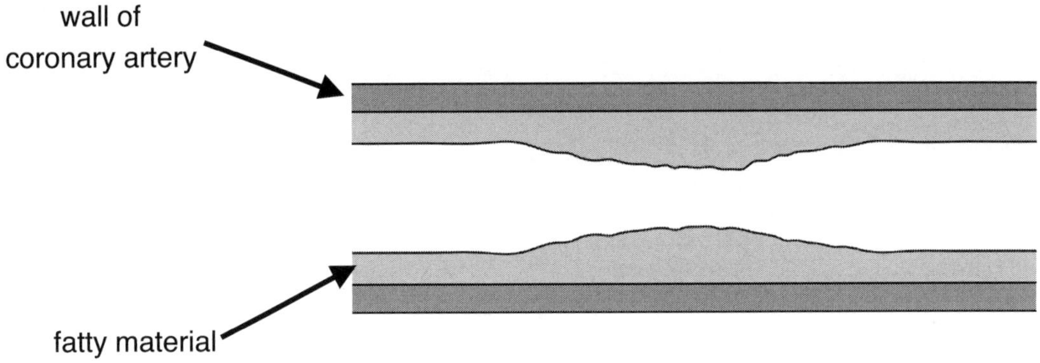


**5 . 5** Narrowing of the coronary artery can be treated with a stent.

Describe how a stent is used to treat a narrowed coronary artery. **2 marks**

______________________________________________

______________________________________________

______________________________________________

______________________________________________

______________________________________________

People who are at a high risk of coronary heart disease can take drugs called statins.

**5 . 6** Describe how statins reduce the risk of coronary heart disease. **2 marks**

______________________________________________

______________________________________________

______________________________________________

______________________________________________

______________________________________________

______________________________________________

**5 . 7** Like all drugs, statins were tested in a double blind trial against a placebo.

State what is meant by the following terms.

**4 marks**

Placebo

______________________________________________________________________

______________________________________________________________________

Double blind trial

______________________________________________________________________

______________________________________________________________________

**Total = 17**

Printed in Great Britain
by Amazon

33521842R00066